Hanauma Bay

A MARINE LIFE GUIDE
to Hawai'i's Most Popular Nature Preserve

Text and photos by
JOHN P. HOOVER

Mutual Publishing

Library of Congress Cataloging Card Number:
2001097901

ISBN 1-56647-531-7

Design by Sistenda Yim

First Printing, May 2002

Mutual Publishing
1215 Center Street, Suite 210
Honolulu, Hawai'i 96816
Telephone (808) 732-1709
Fax (808)734-4094
Email: mutual@lava.net
www.mutualpublishing.com

Printed in Korea

TABLE OF CONTENTS

Jeff Kuwabara and Alan Hong (Hanauma Bay Nature Preserve) answered endless questions about the bay. Jeff reviewed much of the manuscript. Jim Howe, Chief of Lifeguard Operations for the City and County of Honolulu, briefed me on safety. Most of the tips in the safety chapter are his.

Dr. Ralph Moberly (University of Hawai'i at Mānoa) provided reference materials and helped me understand Hanauma Bay's geology. Eric Grossman (University of Hawai'i) explained sea level changes.

Dr. Alan D. Chave (Woods Hole Oceanographic Institution) answered questions about undersea cables. Dan Dickey made numerous dives with me in the bay to trace the routes of cables, record depths, and verify details.

Dr. John E. Randall (Bernice Pauahi Bishop Museum) and Bruce C. Mundy (National Marine Fisheries Service) provided essential information on fishes. Dr. Randall's book, *Shore Fishes of Hawai'i,* was an indispensable reference.

Keith Leber edited the manuscript and checked all scientific and Hawaiian names. With his logical mind, fine sense of language, and knowledge of natural history, Keith improved the book in many ways.

Suzanne Hammer, Sally Drake, and Betty and Al Leach, regular early-morning snorkelers at the bay, showed me their favorite spots. Suzanne reported unusual finds via photographs and email, and answered many questions.

Brenda Timas (Air Survey Hawai'i) and Brent McGee (www.shorediving.com) provided the aerial photos on which the underwater map is based. Capt. Gary R. Layne (University of Hawai'i) flew me over the bay to shoot more photos. Blu Forman (www.bluforman.com) created the map.

Dave Schrichte (Schrichte's Underwater Photo), who probably knows the bay underwater better than anyone else, made his extensive collection of photos available.

Douglas Peebles provided the photos of Hanauma Bay on pages 25 and 28.

Mike Markrich and Jack Sidener (University of Hawai'i at Mānoa) helped me track down the elusive source of the James Jones story.

Jose Orantes encouraged me daily to keep writing.

Marcia Stone, my lovely wife, supported me in every way. When we snorkeled together she always spotted something interesting that I didn't see.

This field guide presents 117 fish species likely to be seen by snorkelers in the shallow waters of Oʻahu's Hanauma Bay Nature Preserve. It also covers sea turtles and 37 species of corals and other marine invertebrates. Although written specifically for Hanauma Bay, it will be useful to snorkelers anywhere in Hawaiʻi.

Most of the photographs were taken in Hanauma Bay specifically for this book. Much of the text, however, has been adapted from my larger books, *Hawaiʻi's Fishes* and *Hawaiʻi's Sea Creatures*. If you are a scuba diver, free diver, or advanced snorkeler you will find those volumes useful as well.

Hanauma Bay is a marvelous place to watch marine life. The inner waters are calm, the fish plentiful and unafraid, and the setting spectacular. (You will be snorkeling in a drowned volcanic crater!) Do not expect a lush, colorful coral reef such as you might see in the Caribbean or Western Pacific, but do plan to have a great time getting up close to some fascinating and colorful animals.

To get you started, here is some basic information:

- Hanauma Bay Nature Preserve is about 10 miles east of Waikīkī just off the main coastal road (Kalanianaʻole Highway, Route 72). Currently it is open every day except Tuesday from 6 AM to 6 PM (winter) and 6 AM to 7 PM (summer). Changes are possible at any time; for the latest information call the recorded information line at 396-4229.

- Plan to get to the bay early. The parking lot often fills by 10 AM and you will be turned away if it is full. By getting an extra early start you will avoid long lines at the ticket booth and snorkel concession.

- If you aren't driving you can catch the number 22 bus from Waikīkī. It runs down Kuhio Avenue every half hour, starting at 8:15 AM. For more information call TheBus at 848-5555.

- The current fees at Hanauma Bay are $1.00 per car to park and $3.00 per person to enter. The entrance fee is waived for children under 13 and for residents of Hawaiʻi with identification. Changes are possible at any time; for the latest information call the recorded information line at 396-4229.

- You can rent masks, fins, and snorkels at the beach, but for the best fit (and to avoid lines) bring your own.

- The entire bay is a marine preserve. Feeding the fish and taking or damaging marine life are prohibited. Before you are allowed in the water you will see a video on marine conservation.

- The waters just off the beach are shallow and protected. You don't have to be a good swimmer to enjoy Hanauma but please read the short chapter on safety (below). You can see quite a few fish just by wading.

- For natural reasons, coral is not plentiful in the shallow snorkeling areas inside the reef. Fishes abound, but the reef itself is rather barren and rocky. Coral grows pro-

  fusely outside the reef, but this area is often too rough for enjoyable snorkeling, and the visibility too poor. Most visitors stay inside. For more information on coral see p.162.

- Snorkelers who wish to explore beyond the protected inner reef should be experienced and confident ocean swimmers.

- See p.41-42 for information on ocean conditions and forecasts.

- Hanauma is pronounced "ha-NOW-ma."

SAFETY

Hanauma Bay is not a theme park—it's the real thing. The bay is a dynamic, ever-changing, ever-wonderful, and potentially dangerous environment. Most people have great experiences at Hanauma Bay, many more than those that don't. By using common sense and following these tips you can be one of the former rather than the latter.

- If you do not know how to swim, limit your in-water activities to wading near shore. The Keyhole Lagoon is a good place for this. Don't get in over your head.

- A flotation device is no substitute for knowing how to swim. Non-swimmers can get into trouble when their float gets punctured on rocks or when gusty winds blow their float into areas they'd rather not be in. In rough, choppy seas slippery sunscreens and oils make it hard to stay on.

- Remain *inside* the reef unless you are a strong, confident and experienced ocean swimmer.

- Unless you are an experienced ocean swimmer, stay away from the two channels that lead outside the reef. A surprisingly strong current rips through them, especially at low tide. It can be all too easy to swim out, and difficult to get back in. These channels are sometimes marked by flags. The Telephone Cable Channel, also called the Slot, is approximately in front of the lifeguard tower at the center of the beach. More rescues are made here than in any other part of the bay. The second channel, the Back Door, is at the seaward end of the Back Door Lagoon at the far left end of the beach.

• Swimming and snorkeling are different skills. If you plan to snorkel, make sure you know how to use your equipment.

• Small children, even if they are good swimmers, need constant adult supervision. This is especially true if they are new to snorkeling. Hanauma Bay is a family place. Families should stay together.

• Do not walk or clamber about on top of the reef. It is riddled with openings and holes, many of them deep. Non-swimmers have had to be rescued after falling into water that is over their heads.

• Moray eels live in the snorkeling areas, some quite large. They are not normally aggressive toward humans but will bite hands placed in or near the holes in which they are hiding. Bites from even small eels can be serious, often tearing ligaments or damaging nerves. Do not put your hands in or around holes. It's best to keep your hands at your sides while snorkeling.

• From shore it is difficult to judge conditions outside the reef. The sea is often rougher than it appears. If you plan to swim or snorkel outside the reef, inquire about conditions at the information kiosk. Or ask a lifeguard. Only confident, experienced ocean swimmers should snorkel beyond the reef (beyond the line of breaking waves).

• If you venture outside the reef, stay away from the shallow areas along the reef's outside edge. Breaking waves can wash you over the rocks causing scrapes and injuries.

• The sides of the bay are steep, rocky and turbulent. Only a few places exist where a tired swimmer can climb out. Unless you know exactly where these are (and few visitors do), plan to enter and exit the water from the beach. Don't jump into the water from the ledges along the sides of the bay unless you are an experienced ocean swimmer capable of swimming back to the beach.

• The wide ledges on each side of the bay (Toilet Bowl Ledge and Witch's Brew Ledge) can be dangerous during periods of strong wind and waves. Park management closes the ledges whenever conditions are marginal. Respect these closures. In the past large waves have knocked people down, bruising and lacerating them, or even washing them into the sea. If you walk the ledges stay on dry rock as much as possible. Wet areas are the areas regularly splashed by waves.

- Be careful at the Toilet Bowl, a small, deep, active pool around the point at the left side of the bay. (You are out of sight of the lifeguards from here and it's a long way back. Bring a cell phone if you have one.) The area immediately around the pool can be extremely slippery and accidents there are common. The pool itself is connected to the sea by a narrow tunnel, causing it to fill and empty with the waves. Daredevils enjoy jumping in, but when the surf is up the pool can be violent. The sudden inflow of water can throw people onto the rocks, and the "flushing" action can be frightening to those who enter unprepared. Some panic. If in doubt, stay out of the Toilet Bowl. Above all, never attempt to swim through the narrow passage connecting it with the ocean.

- The Witch's Brew is an aptly named area beyond the point of land halfway out along the right side of the bay (Witch's Brew Point). Exposed to the tradewind swell, it is rough and choppy and accumulates an unappealing assortment of floating debris. Unless it's a flat calm day, stay out of the Witch's Brew.

- Do not clamber about on the cliffs above the bay. Loose crumbly rocks make it all too easy to slip and fall.

- *Oh yes.... don't forget the sunscreen!*

A SHORT HISTORY OF HANAUMA BAY

Hanauma Bay's volcanic origins are easily seen from the air. Koko Head, a compound cone containing two craters, rises south of the bay. The Koko Head craters, filled with vegetation, mirror the two larger water-filled Hanauma craters. The road marks the rim of an even larger, more ancient crater in which Hanauma Bay is nested.

Geology

The volcanic island of O'ahu first emerged from the sea amid lava and steam perhaps three million years ago. A second volcano broke the surface somewhat to the east about a million years later. The twin volcanoes—perhaps the earth's largest at the time—eventually joined to form a single island. In time they cooled. Streams cut valleys down their slopes, forests clothed them, and coral reefs grew along their shores. When eruptions ceased, possibly a million years ago, O'ahu was considerably larger and higher than it is today. Waves, rain, and wind gnawed at the land, and vast landslides carved huge chunks from its flanks. Eventually the two giant volcanoes became so cut up and eroded that they no longer looked like single mountains. We know them today as the Wai'anae and Ko'olau mountain ranges.

Although greatly altered and apparently extinct, the ancient volcanoes still harbored pockets of molten rock deep within. From time to time, perhaps as a result of earthquakes or shifting land, this magma forced its way to the surface through fissures and cracks. When such cracks opened 125,000 or more years ago under present-day Honolulu, hot magma contacted sea water creating violent steam and ash explosions. These formed large craters and cones such as the familiar landmarks Diamond Head and Punchbowl. (Sea level at the time was higher, explaining why some of these formations are now well inland.)

Hanauma Bay and 1,200-ft. Koko Crater, as seen from Koko Head.

The south side of Hanauma Bay seen from the ridge behind the Toilet Bowl. The "rainbow" formation may mark the location of an old crater wall, now completely eroded away.

Steam and ash explosions from a fissure off O'ahu's southeastern tip created a new peninsula with similar formations perhaps as recently as 35,000 years ago, when sea level was lower.[1] Most conspicuous among these formations are Koko Crater, a deeply furrowed cone 1,200 ft. high, and Koko Head, the 600-ft. compound remains of several large cones that resemble

---

[1]Age estimates for the last eruption on southeastern O'ahu vary from 31,000 to 320,000 years. The ages of Diamond Head, Punchbowl, and even O'ahu itself are also in dispute.

the sloping back of an immense whale from the Honolulu side. One of the eruptions blasted an unusually low, wide crater, then shifted to form a second crater partially overlapping the first. The double crater's southeast side bordered the sea, which was notably lower than it is today. (All this occurred during an ice age when a considerable amount of the Earth's water was frozen in vast glaciers.) As the earth warmed, sea levels rose. In due time, ocean waves broke through the low southeast crater wall (if one existed), washing it completely away.[2] Eventually the rising sea flooded the double crater, creating a horseshoe-shaped bay about a quarter of a mile wide and half a mile deep—the bay we call Hanauma.

The bay's protected waters were ideal for the growth of corals and limestone-depositing coralline algae, which began building a reef along the bay's innermost edge. Sea level continued to rise and the fringing reef grew upward and outward. Radiocarbon dating of cores drilled through this reef reveal that the oldest layer of limestone formed about 7,000 years ago—fixing the approximate date of the flood that created the bay.

The soft, brown, layered stone that forms the walls of Hanauma Bay, Koko Head, and this entire corner of O'ahu is called tuff. Tuff results when magma and sea water explode into light

Bits of white coral and black basalt, fragmented during the eruption, remain embedded in the brown tuff walls of Hanauma Bay. Above lie several small basalt bombs. Thrown high in the air, they depressed the surrounding ash when they landed.

A large volcanic bomb of reef limestone partially exposed in the gully behind the Toilet Bowl. Note the downward sag of the surrounding ash layers, now hardened into tuff.

---

[2]A southeast wall may never have formed at Hanauma, possibly because strong easterly winds prevented ash from accumulating on that side, or because the submarine slope was too steep to support a stable wall. Nearby Koko Crater lacks a wall on its northeast side.

Basalt bombs landing on the crater rim "plopped" into the still soft ash creating cow-pie-like formations.

Greenish olivine sand near the Toilet Bowl. Much of Hanauma's main beach was originally this color, as is much of the sand at the bottom of the bay.

volcanic ash, which later consolidates into rock. Look closely at the tuff around the edge of the bay and you will see embedded bits of white coral, the remains of ancient coral heads torn apart by the undersea eruptions. Small pieces of dark basalt, blasted from the original underlying rock, are also present. Volcanic bombs—larger chunks of basalt, limestone, or older tuff thrown high in the air—landed in the soft ash creating formations called bomb sags. Bomb sags are common on nearby Koko Head and on the ridge beyond the Toilet Bowl (actually the rim of an even older crater in which the Hanauma craters are nested). They resemble cow pies with a stone in the center. You can also see partially eroded sags in the walls of the bay. A particularly large limestone bomb lies partially exposed in the gully behind the Toilet Bowl. Notice how the layers of tuff were depressed by the weight of the falling rock, which penetrated at least five feet into the ash.

The tuff near the beach at Hanauma contains small greenish crystals of the mineral olivine. Hard and heavy, the olivine crystals accumulate after the tuff matrix wears away, giving a green tint to the sand. Hanauma Bay once had one of the few "green sand" beaches in Hawai'i, and perhaps in the world. White sand brought in to extend and replenish the beach over the years has all but obliterated it. Traces of sparkling greenish olivine sand remain at the far right end of the beach; there is more at the Toilet Bowl, a wave-fed pool located around the point at the left side of the bay that fills and empties through an underground connection to the sea.

At the edges of Hanauma Bay lies a ledge, or bench, 3 to 10 ft. above sea level and up to 20 ft. wide. This ledge has long puzzled geologists, who at first believed that waves carved it

The ledge or bench around the sides of Hanauma Bay continues to widen today. The large blocks of tuff fell from above when the material beneath them eroded away. Splashing waves keep the tuff near the waterline wet and hard. Above the splash line it erodes more easily.

Reddish basalt above the arch looks almost fluid, as if recently cooled.

This natural arch formed when soft tuff eroded beneath the harder basalt of a small lava flow that cascaded down the crater wall from a vent higher up.

when sea level was higher. Today, most geologists consider the present action of the sea responsible. Tuff remains cemented and hard wherever it is kept wet; thus close to sea level it resists erosion. Above the splash line, where the tuff is alternately wetted and dried (mostly by ground water percolating through after occasional heavy rains), it rapidly disintegrates. This weathering created the bench, which continues to widen today.

When wave-action is light, you can safely walk along the bench all the way around Toilet Bowl Point at the left side of the bay. On the way you will have to climb through a small natural arch under some hard black basalt. This small lava flow formed when molten rock poured over the already eroded crater wall from a vent just to the northwest. Above the hole is some reddish basalt that looks almost fluid, as if recently congealed. Large blocks and boulders of tuff lying on the bench beyond fell from above when the underlying rock disintegrated. In this way the cliffs were formed. As you reach the point, notice that the bench is higher than along the protected sides of the bay. The waves here wash further up on the rocks, keeping more of the tuff wet and hard. The same effect can be seen at the Witch's Brew Point across the bay.

As we have seen, sea level fluctuates. When the original Hanauma craters were formed, the sea was probably several hundred feet lower than it is today; about 3,500 years ago it was about six feet higher. During this high stand of the sea, the coral reef along the inner shore grew to its maximum height, probably reaching to within a few feet of the low tide line. As sea level gradually dropped back to its present position, the top of this fringing reef was increasingly exposed and the coral died. Wave action leveled and flattened the coral heads, forming the foundation of the shallow limestone reef flat that today extends about 250-300 ft. seaward of the present beach. This is essentially a fossil coral reef covered with layers of limestone deposited by crustose coralline algae (see p.195). Like the original coral reef, it is riddled with crevices and holes where fish and other animals live and take shelter.

In structure this reef resembles a coral reef, but because living coral is so sparse on its surface (about one percent of the total area), someone conceived the idea that people killed all the coral by walking on it. The story took hold and was repeated so widely and for so many years in the media and in books that it is now "common knowledge." Actually, the barrenness is natural. Live coral can

Hanauma Bay's fringing reef is a fossil coral reef overgrown by limestone-depositing coralline algae. The original coral died centuries ago after sea level dropped to its present level. Much of the complex structure of the original reef remains. The seaward edge, called the "algal ridge," is highest. It is seen here almost completely exposed during a very low tide.

scarcely grow on such a shallow, exposed reef top, but various species of algae thrive, especially the limestone-depositing coralline algae mentioned above that created much of the reef we now see.[3] These algae form hard rocky crusts that are tan, pinkish, or purplish. They do not look like ordinary seaweed.

The reef's most common species of coralline algae thrives where wave action is strongest, thus the seaward edge of the reef has grown the highest. This "algal ridge," almost completely exposed at low tide, absorbs most of the force of the waves, protecting the beach and the back areas. Herbivorous fishes in the bay keep the surfaces of the reef flat grazed almost bare of larger seaweeds and other fleshy algae.

Heads of living coral—yellowish brown, grayish brown and greenish—start to become common just seaward of the algal ridge, growing larger and more numerous as depth increases. The corals in Hanauma Bay are some of the healthiest and most diverse in Hawai'i. Intermediate and advanced snorkelers who venture outside the inner reef will find parts of the bay floor almost completely covered with massive mounds of Lobe Coral, colorful patches of Rice Coral, Blue Rice Coral and Spreading Coral, and in deeper water stands of branching Finger Coral. It is not necessary, however, to leave the shelter of the inner reef to see living corals. Novice snorkelers can find modest colonies of at least 12 species along the sides of the natural pools and lagoons. Living corals are unmistakably brown, yellow-brown, or even blue and their textures are very different from the rocky, algae-covered limestone that makes up most of the reef flat.

Hawaiian History

The climate at Hanauma Bay is hot and dry. Because there is no fresh water it is unlikely that anyone lived at the bay in ancient times, but Hawaiians certainly fished there. In 1952, archeologists excavating a shelter cave behind the beach found remnants of ancient campfires, fishhooks, and other tools. The bay and the volcanic formations around it also figure in old Hawaiian legends, and there are several accounts of how Hanauma Bay got its name. The word **hana** means "bay." The word **uma** has several meanings, one being "curved." One translation of **Hanauma** is therefore "curved bay," certainly appropriate. (The name is pronounced "Ha-now-ma," with the accent on "now.")

Uma also connotes the curved stern of a canoe. The sheltered bay was a traditional place for canoes to gather, waiting for favorable winds before crossing the rough channel to Moloka'i, and it was a landing place for canoes coming from Moloka'i. The high hill to the right of the bay as one faces seaward, known today as Koko Head, was a lookout point called in old times Mo'okua-o-Kaneapua. From its top one can see the islands of Moloka'i, Lāna'i, and on a very clear day, even West Maui and Haleakalā. Travelers would climb this hill to view sea and wind conditions before attempting to cross the channel.

Finally, **uma** means "hand-wrestling." In this game two players knelt facing each other with one elbow on the ground. Each clasped his opponent's right hand and tried to force the other's arm

---

[3]So prevalent and unchallenged was the belief that human trampling killed the reef that in the late 1990s the City and County of Honolulu almost funded a strange scheme to construct an aquarium on the rim of the bay so that visitors could view sea life without endangering it. The plan would have restricted access to the beach and required snorkelers to be accompanied by a guide. Public outcry quickly killed that proposal but some of the money was used to build the present education center.

down. After Kamehameha conquered Oʻahu in 1795, his wife Queen Kaʻahumanu visited the bay. History records that hula dancers and hand-wrestlers entertained her. "Women joined in and a whole month was spent there," wrote the chronicler. "That was why the place was called Hana-uma." Another story, of uncertain origin, relates that two warriors fell in love with the same woman. They hand-wrestled each other at the bay to decide who could marry her, but neither could best his opponent. Fearing the rivals would harm themselves, the woman turned herself into the beautiful mountain we now call Koko Crater so that each could gaze on her beauty forever. Her father, taking the form of an immense lizard or dragon (mo'o), curled himself at the foot of Koko Crater to protect her, forming the arms of Hanauma Bay.

With the advent of the Kingdom of Hawaiʻi, the lands around Hanauma became the property of King Kamehameha I. For many years thereafter the bay was the favorite fishing camp of Hawaiian royalty—King Kamehameha V and Prince Jonah Kuhio disported themselves there, among others. In 1883, Hanauma Bay and surrounding lands came into the possession of Bernice Pauahi Bishop, and later her estate, known today as Kamehameha Schools.

Modern History

Modest development at Hanauma Bay began before the turn of the century. A photograph taken in the 1890s shows a building on the beach, perhaps constructed for the use of royalty. (The beach in the picture is somewhat narrower than the beach today.) A 1918 magazine article about Oʻahu's arid southeast side mentions that water was available at Hanauma for thirsty travelers. In 1928, the City and County of Honolulu established Koko Head Regional Park—the land encompassing Koko Head, Hanauma Bay, and Koko Crater—by buying it for one dollar from the estate of Bernice Pauahi Bishop. A deed restriction limited its use to public parks and rights of way. Around 1931 a new paved road replaced the old track around southeast Oʻahu and a steep walkway with safety rails was installed at Hanauma for the convenience of the few beachgoers who ventured this far from town. In 1941, shortly after the bombing of Pearl Harbor, the U.S. Army strung barbed wire along the beach and stationed soldiers there to repel a possible Japanese invasion. (Among the few remnants of this occupation is a collapsed but still well-camouflaged bunker near the Toilet Bowl. It takes a sharp eye to spot it.)[4] After the war, in 1950, the City and County of Honolulu built a road to the beach and installed new restrooms and showers. Hanauma Bay quickly became a favorite fishing and picnicking park for residents of Honolulu. Swimming at Hanauma, however, was difficult. Except for the two natural lagoons at the north end of the beach, an almost unbroken expanse of shallow reef fringed the shore. A photo from this period shows a narrow channel running through the reef flat, possibly dug at this time to allow swimmers to reach deeper water.

---

[4]The story that troops dynamited the reef to create a swimming hole apparently originates in a 1974 magazine article by James Jones, author of the novel *From Here to Eternity*. Jones had been stationed at Hanauma. Revisiting Hawaiʻi for the first time after the war, he recounts stopping at the bay and notes "The reef was exactly the same as I remembered. The hole we had blasted in it to enlarge the swimming area was still there." Based on this, a few Oʻahu guidebooks have suggested that the Army created the large break in the reef known as the Keyhole. A photograph from the 1890s, however, shows the Keyhole area much as it is today. The location of the hole Jones described is unknown.

Hanauma Bay's fringing reef in 1937. Except for the two natural lagoons at the left end of the beach (not in the picture) an almost unbroken expanse of shallow reef fringed the shore making swimming difficult. (Hawai'i State Archives)

Blasting the reef in 1956 to lay the first trans-Pacific undersea telephone cable. An artificial swimming area was created at the same time. (Bernice Pauahi Bishop Museum)

The reef today. Much of the central portion has been cleared as an artificial swimming area. A pile of black boulders protects it from the sea. A second swimming area blasted in 1970 can be seen in the distance.

In 1956, the City and County of Honolulu sold the Hawaiian Telephone Company an easement through the bay for the first leg of a new trans-Pacific undersea telephone cable.[5] Barges, trucks, and bulldozers were brought in. The contractor, Hawaiian Dredging, blasted a 200-ft. wide swath through the reef. Tons of coral rock were piled on the beach and removed. Oil covered the water. In a matter of days the central portion of Hanauma's beautiful fringing reef, and some of the reef beyond, had been destroyed forever. Such devastation would be unthinkable today, but in those times it was considered an improvement   the public now had more swimming space. On the positive side, the dynamiting and dredging created a new biological zone inside the reef. Loose rubble left by the blasting became habitat for a host of small invertebrates and the fishes that feed on them, many of which had probably not lived inside the reef in any numbers before. The swimming area (knee- to chest-deep at low tide) gave these fishes ample living space. The channel provided a way in and out, as well as improving water circulation inside the reef. Quite a few species occur today in the artificial swimming area that do not occur in the natural sandy-bottomed lagoons.

With more places to swim and easier access to deep water, Hanauma Bay increased in popularity. Many residents fished there and by the 1960s few fish of any size were left. In 1967, and not without opposition, the State Division of Fish and Game declared the entire bay a Marine Life Conservation District, prohibiting the taking of marine life, shells, coral, rocks, or sand. One problem remained: surf entering through the wide cable channel was eroding the

[5]The 2,400-mile twin cables (one to send, one to receive) eventually terminated at Point Arena, California, and were at the time the world's longest undersea cables. In use until 1989, they are still in place. The cables, now largely covered over, run under the boulder reef. Two more cables, laid in 1964, run through the telephone cable channel just to the right of the boulder reef. One, apparently abandoned, ends in the sand in the middle of the bay. The other runs around Pai'olu'olu Point 56 miles to Mākaha. It remained in use until 1987. See map on p. 24.

beach. In 1970, the City Dept. of Parks and Recreation remedied this by partially blocking the channel with an artificial reef of heavy basalt boulders. (The top of this boulder pile is easily seen from shore at low tide.) As part of the same project, and in spite of some community opposition, the City blasted and dredged more reef on the right side of the bay to create a second swimming area in front of the far restroom. Workers buried the dredgings under the beach and covered them with 4,000 cubic feet of white sand brought in from O'ahu's north shore. As before, the blasting and dredging created a rubble bottom in which many small animals could live and increased the habitat for larger fishes inside the reef. Also, the new boulder pile sheltered the original swimming area from incoming waves, making it more habitable for marine life. Its outer face became one of the best shallow snorkeling areas outside the reef.

Now prohibited, fish feeding was for many years a popular activity at Hanauma Bay. Current park policy favors keeping the reef as natural as possible.

After creation of the marine preserve, snorkeling and fish feeding at Hanauma became hugely popular. Tourists brought in by the busload soon began to outnumber residents on the beach. To make room for everyone the City built an additional parking lot, and by the late 1980s as many as 10,000 people per day were using the bay. The number of fish in the natural lagoons and artificial swimming areas increased enormously as people fed them bread, peas, and human snack foods. Tossing a handful of fish food into the water caused it to boil with fishes large and small. It was thrilling to stand waist deep with fast-moving animals swirling around—most visitors had never been so close to wild creatures.

Although fish feeding was popular and exciting, park officials began to suspect that human foods might be bad for the fish. To improve their nutrition, the snack shop sold handy little bags of commercial trout chow, and Park officials encouraged its use. But there were other considerations. Large chubs and surgeonfishes from the deeper waters of the bay, entering the inner areas to be fed, were altering what was perceived as the natural species composition of the inner reef. An occasional overly eager fish would bite a child's hand, sometimes even drawing blood. Finally, a 1999 City ordinance banned fish feeding entirely.

Fish feeding, of course, was not the only problem. The beach and nearshore waters were over-crowded. Visitors left their vehicles on the lawn, on the roadways, and on the highway. Commercial tours were monopolizing the picnic facilities. It was out of control. Also, many people believed at the time that beachgoers were killing the coral by walking on it. Although unsubstantiated, this environmental concern prompted action. Around 1990 park authorities began a program to minimize impact on the bay both by reducing the number of visitors and by teaching conservation. Most commercial activities were banned and stricter controls on parking were put in place. When the lot filled, cars were turned away. Meanwhile, a volunteer organization, the Friends of Hanauma Bay, working from a booth on the beach, taught thousands of visitors to care for and appreciate marine life. In 1998 the City began charging admission and parking fees, further reducing the number of visitors. The program was a success, albeit with an unforeseen consequence: local people came in fewer numbers and Hanauma Bay became largely a tourist destination. Park officials hope to reverse this.

In 1999 the City began a three-year carrying capacity study to determine the number of visitors that is environmentally safe. Happily, preliminary results released in June 2000 suggested that beachgoers and snorkelers have had little detrimental effect on marine life. Besides fish feeding, which has ceased, the study identified only a few minor negative impacts: runoff from freshwater showers, and swimmers not using restrooms. It was too soon to determine whether people walking on the reef flat over the years had significantly altered or damaged it.

About 3,000 people now visit Hanauma Bay Nature Preserve each day, making it one of the most visited beaches in the State. To keep the marine environment as natural as possible without further lowering the visitor count, the City and County of Honolulu has moved the snack bar up from the beach, built a new Education Center, and instituted a mandatory training video for first-time visitors. All beachgoers now hear a clear message of preservation, conservation, and safety before entering the water.

Today the City and County of Honolulu administers that part of Hanauma Bay Nature Preserve lying above the high tide line, and the State of Hawai'i Dept. of Land and Natural Resources manages the underwater portion.

ISOLATION AND ENDEMISM

Hawai'i is a wonderful place to snorkel, not only because of the warm, clear water but also because about 25 percent of the marine animals are endemic—they occur nowhere else. Few locations compare with Hawai'i in number of unique fish and invertebrate species, and none has more. How did our marine animals originally get here? Where did they come from? Let's take a closer look.

Scientists believe that most tropical marine life—even that of the tropical Atlantic and Caribbean—originated in the ancient warm seas around Indonesia and the Philippines. More species of marine animals are found in these waters than anywhere else, and their number decreases markedly as one moves away. Shallow-water animals and plants have spread slowly from this center of dispersal, moving from island to island or along the shores of continents. Pacific island groups, lying close together, tend to form series of "stepping stones" along which animals and plants can disperse. The Hawaiian Islands, however, are separated from all other Pacific islands by distances of more than 1,000 miles (discounting tiny Johnston Island lying to the south). This gap, greater than the distance between other Pacific islands and their neighbors, is probably the most important factor influencing the composition of Hawai'i's marine fauna.

Almost all marine animals begin life as minute drifting larvae. Carried varying distances by ocean currents, they eventually settle to the ocean floor or in some other habitat to mature. The ancestors of most Hawaiian reef and shore animals arrived here the same way—as drifting larvae. But so isolated were these island waters that only species with long-lasting larval stages survived the journey. Those with brief larval stages died in the open sea. Distance acted as a filter.

Crossing the gap was only the first challenge. Having arrived in Hawaiian waters, a species still had to find favorable habitat and suitable food. Lacking these it would quickly perish. To reproduce, it had to arrive in numbers sufficient for males and females to mature at the same time and find each other. Because of these winnowing effects, far fewer marine species occur in Hawai'i than in Indo-Pacific locations such as French Polynesia, Micronesia, Australia, Thailand, or even far-away East Africa. Indeed, whole groups of animals common in those areas are absent from the Hawaiian shallow-water fauna. Among the fishes that never reached Hawai'i, for example, are the colorful anemonefishes, found almost everywhere else in the tropical Indo-Pacific. Anemonefishes never reached Hawai'i because their larval stage lasts only about a week. Moray eels and surgeonfishes, on the other hand, drift as larvae for months and are here in abundance.

Isolation, however, has worked two ways. Although impoverishing Hawai'i's fauna on one hand, it has enriched it on the other. The great distance between Hawai'i and other islands made possible the emergence of many new species. About 20 percent of Hawaiian marine invertebrates and 25 percent of Hawaiian fishes are unique to the Islands. Most of these probably evolved from Indo-Pacific ancestors that arrived by chance in the distant past. Species limited to a relatively small geographical area are called **endemics**. A few endemics are relict species, unusual species whose evolutionary line appears to have died out everywhere else.

Isolation encourages endemism because small, confined populations are easily affected by genetic changes. Favorable mutations spread quickly through the gene pool, organisms become progressively better adapted to their environment and, given enough time, often evolve characteristics distinct from those of their ancestors. The Hawaiian Sergeant *(Abudefduf abdominalis)* is a good example. Although similar to its Indo-Pacific cousin *(A. vaigiensis)*, it differs sufficiently in color pattern and other details to be considered a separate Hawaiian species. Only a few other places in the world have a percentage of endemic animals comparable to Hawai'i's. Easter Island, also very isolated, is one of these; the Red Sea region, isolated not by distance but by geology, is another.

Over the years the list of Hawaiian endemics has changed considerably. Some species formerly considered endemic have been dropped as their wider geographic range has become known; others, newly discovered, have been added. In this book, Hawaiian endemics are marked with a red dot. (•)

In addition to the endemics, there exist a number of Hawaiian sea animals that differ distinctly in size, color, or other details from members of the same species elsewhere. In Hawai'i, for example, males of the Spotted Boxfish *(Ostracion meleagris)* have few or no gold spots on their sides. Elsewhere in the Indo-Pacific their sides are covered with gold spots. Sometimes such animals are classified as subspecies. This is the case with the boxfish in Hawai'i, which bears the subspecies name *camurum*.

Another characteristic of Hawaiian reefs is the abundance of certain animals that are uncommon everywhere else. Red Pencil Urchins *(Heterocentrotus mammillatus)* occur sparsely throughout the Indo-Pacific but in Hawai'i can be plentiful, adding bright red splashes of color to our reefs. Perhaps their predators and competitors had brief larval stages and were left behind. Another colorful animal abundant in Hawai'i and not very common elsewhere is the Yellow Tang *(Zebrasoma flavescens)*.

The careful observer is sure to find many other differences between Hawaiian marine animals and their counterparts elsewhere in the Indo-Pacific.

The Bluestripe Butterflyfish is a Hawaiian endemic that resembles no other known butterflyfish. Species such as this, whose ancestors and relatives are extinct, are known as relict species.

The Hawaiian Sergeant occurs only in Hawai'i but resembles others of its genus from the Indo-Pacific and Atlantic. It is closely related to the species below.

The Indo-Pacific Sergeant, probable ancestor of the Hawaiian Sergeant, occurs throughout most of the Indo-Pacific. It has recently established itself in Hawai'i, perhaps drifting in with floating fishing debris, and is not uncommon in Hanauma Bay. Will the two interbreed or remain distinct? Only time will tell.

Hawaiʻi

Indonesia

In Hawaiʻi, male Spotted Boxfish have few or no gold spots on the sides (top). Elsewhere in the Indo-Pacific males have many gold spots on the sides (bottom). The two populations are considered distinct subspecies.

The Red Pencil Urchin occurs throughout the tropical Indo-Pacific but is abundant only in Hawai'i.

Yellow Tangs occur from Hawai'i to southern Japan but are plentiful only here. Perhaps because they are intensively collected for the aquarium trade, Hanauma Bay is one of the few places where large schools of these lovely fish still occur. Photo: D.R. & T.L. Schrichte

ENVIRONMENT AND HABITAT
What Is a Reef?

Hawaiian shores offer a variety of habitats or biological zones. In Hanauma Bay we can divide them roughly into the inner and outer reef areas (often simply referred to as "inside the reef" and "outside the reef"). We can further subdivide these areas into other specific habitats.

But first, what exactly is a reef? A dictionary might define it as "a line or ridge of rocks lying at or near the surface of the water." (If the "rocks" are coral heads, or are covered with corals, the reef would usually be called a **coral reef**.) Ocean scientists and divers, however, often broaden the definition of reef to include rock and coral formations that do not rise all the way to the surface.

Using the broader definition there are a number of reefs in Hanauma Bay (see p. 24). Using the narrow definition there is only one: the inner reef fringing the beach, generally called "the reef." Technically, it is a reef flat, a shallow platform of old coral limestone that fronts the beach and extends seaward about 250-300 ft. Breaking waves usually mark the slightly raised ridge or crest that forms its outer boundary.

Is this inner reef a coral reef? Yes and no. Some visitors, led to believe that they will see a living coral reef, are puzzled and disappointed at the obvious lack of living coral. Calling it a "fossil coral reef" or "coralline algae reef" might be more accurate. Coral animals created its foundations thousands of years ago at a time when sea level was higher (see p. 7). Since then, declining sea levels have made the inner reef inhospitable to living corals, which can now barely survive on its shallow and exposed surface. In their place, tiny limestone-secreting plants called coralline algae have taken over the job of reef-building. Most of this reef's rocky surface is the product of these plants, which thrive in shallow areas where corals cannot easily grow.

The top of the inner reef flat lies a few inches to three feet under water, depending on tide and location. Its raised outer edge, the so-called "algal ridge," breaks the energy of incoming waves, protecting the waters inside. The reef flat is cut by numerous intersecting channels and holes. At the far left end of the beach it opens into two large, natural, sandy-bottomed lagoons with maximum depths of about 10 ft. These lagoons, channels, holes, and a few natural deep pools originally provided most of the habitat for fishes and other animals inside the reef.

During the 1950s, 60s and 70s parts of this inner reef habitat were greatly altered. On at least three occasions the reef flat was blasted and dredged to lay undersea telephone cables, to create artificial swimming areas, or both. The idea, in part, was to make room for beachgoers, but fish and invertebrates moved in as well. The new rubble-and-sand bottom created by the blasting became a habitat for species of animals that likely did not live inside the reef in significant numbers before.

More than 100 species of fish now make the inner reef their home or enter it regularly from deeper water. An undetermined number of invertebrate animals such as crabs, worms, snails, sea cucumbers, and corals live there as well. In this book, when we say "inside the reef" we mean this area—everything inside the line of breaking waves. It corresponds to Zone One (described in the chapter Snorkeling in Hanauma Bay, p. 25) and is where the vast majority of visitors to the bay wade, swim, and snorkel. It contains rocky areas, sandy areas, and areas of mixed rubble and sand, each with its own mix of animals.

A Green Turtle cruises the shallow surge habitat near the outer entrance to the bay. The dominant coral here is Cauliflower Coral. Photo: D.R. & T.L. Schrichte

Biological Zones

Outside Hanauma's fringing reef lie other biological zones, or habitats. One is the shallow, turbulent **surge habitat**, which occurs along the sides of the bay and along the ocean side of the reef flat where the waves break. The surge habitat is characterized by rocky substrate (tuff or coralline algae) with scant coral and ample fleshy algae, a feast for fishes agile enough to survive the crashing waves. Surge habitat specialists include algae-eating surgeonfishes, damselfishes, and blennies. Invertebrate animals specialized for clinging tightly to rocks live here too. One such area lies along the ocean side of the artificial boulder reef, built in 1970 to protect the beach from erosion. This boulder breakwater is easily seen from shore, especially at low tide.

Beyond the surge habitat, in slightly deeper water and where the bottom is hard, lies the **Lobe Coral habitat**, named for the dominant coral species, *Porites lobata*. In Hanauma Bay, this habitat extends to a depth of about 30 ft. and corresponds roughly to snorkeling Zone Two. Here, where turbulence is less severe, mounds of living coral cover much of the bottom. Hollow spaces under many of these coral structures provide shelter for fishes and invertebrates. The variety of fish and invertebrate life in this habitat is greater than anywhere else in the bay. One of the best places to explore the Lobe Coral habitat is the area on the right side of the bay just inside Witch's Brew Point.

The deeper **Finger Coral habitat**, starting at about 30 ft. and subject to little wave action, is dominated by more delicate Finger Coral *(Porites compressa)* but also contains much Lobe Coral. It corresponds roughly to snorkeling Zone Three. This habitat, mostly in the center of the bay, is more the realm of divers than snorkelers. When the water is clear, however, snorkelers can look down and identify quite a variety of marine life.

Between the reefs is the **sand habitat**, which looks desertlike but harbors a surprising amount of life, much of it beneath the sand. Because of its depth, the sand habitat is also difficult for snorkelers to access. In some areas rubble replaces sand.

Snorkeling in Lobe Coral habitat. Lobe Coral is the most abundant coral species in the bay. Photo: D.R. & T.L. Schrichte

A reef of Finger Coral in the center of the bay. Most such reefs are too deep for snorkelers. Photo: D.R. & T.L. Schrichte

A school of Pennant Butterflyfish along the drop-off at the outer entrance to Hanauma Bay.

More accessible, but only in calm weather, is the **boulder habitat**, which occurs along the sides of the bay wherever large numbers of blocks and boulders have fallen from above. Massive coral heads are scant here but Cauliflower Coral *(Pocillopora meandrina)*, the dominant species, grows in compact branching heads on top of the blocks and boulders. This habitat is characterized by great numbers of fish, particularly Hawaiian Sergeants and Black Triggerfish, which find shelter in the spaces between and under the boulders. Surgeonfishes also abound, often grazing in large mixed schools.

Finally, the **drop-off habitat** at the outer entrances to the bay is characterized by clear water, currents, and steep slopes or perpendicular walls containing canyons, caves, and unusual rock formations. This is the habitat preferred by plankton-eaters such as Pyramid and Pennant Butterflyfish. Many other reef fishes can also be found along the walls, but the excitement comes from the large schools of chubs, surgeonfishes and butterflyfishes that frequent the area. Occasionally Spotted Eagle Rays and large pelagic (open-ocean) fishes, such as Manta Rays, are seen as well. The drop-off is almost exclusively the domain of the diver, although during exceptionally calm weather advanced snorkelers (strong, confident ocean swimmers equipped with fins) can explore the top of the walls along the outer right side of the bay. There are sometimes currents running parallel to the coast here, so be careful.

Most of the habitat zones in Hanauma Bay are typical of Hawaiian coastal waters in general. Although Hawai'i's underwater environment does not offer the lush exuberance of Micronesian or Caribbean coral reefs, it has a spare beauty of its own in which unique and colorful fishes are the prime attraction.

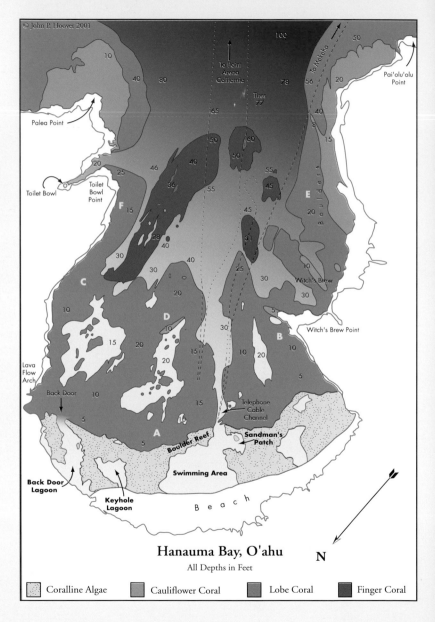

© John P. Hoover 2001

To Point
Arena
California

To Molokai

Pai'olu'olu
Point

Tires

Palea Point

Toilet
Bowl
Point

Toilet Bowl

Boulders

E

F

Witch's Brew

Witch's Brew Point

Lava
Flow
Arch

C

D

B

Back Door

A

Telephone
Cable
Channel

Boulder Reef

Sandman's
Patch

Back Door
Lagoon

Keyhole
Lagoon

Swimming Area

Beach

Hanauma Bay, O'ahu

All Depths in Feet

N

| Coralline Algae | Cauliflower Coral | Lobe Coral | Finger Coral |

SNORKELING IN HANAUMA BAY
Overview

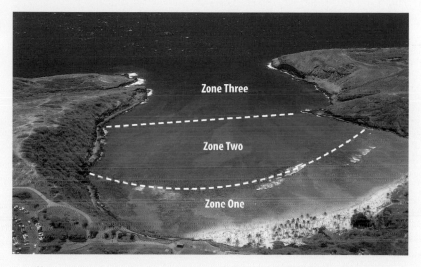

Hanauma Bay can be divided into three snorkeling zones. **Zone One** contains the broad, shallow reef flat and the pools, lagoons, and swimming areas within it. The reef flat extends seaward about 250-300 ft. from shore and dominates the view as you walk down the road to the beach. At its left (northeast) end are two large natural pools or lagoons, the Keyhole Lagoon and the Back Door Lagoon. Fronting the center of the beach is the Swimming Area, created by blasting in the 1950s and 1960s. A second and shallower swimming area created in 1970 lies at the right (south) end of the beach.

Safe and protected, Zone One ("inside the reef") is where most people snorkel. Fish are abundant and there are small colonies of live coral. Two shallow channels, usually with a slight to moderately strong outgoing current, lead outside the reef into Zone Two. The most obvious of these is the Telephone Cable Channel (also called the Slot) which is opposite the lifeguard station at the center of the beach. The other channel, opposite the far left end of the beach, is called the Back Door. Do not venture through these channels unless you are a confident ocean swimmer. Getting out is easy; getting back in can be challenging. For swimmers inside the reef there are no other hazards to speak of (except sunburn) but do not put your hands in holes as they may harbor moray eels. Non-swimmers should confine themselves to wading close to the beach. The deeper parts of the Swimming Area, lagoons and pools are hazardous for non-swimmers, even if a flotation device is used.

Zone Two encompasses the area outside the reef approximately as far as Witch's Brew Point, the rocky point on the right side of the bay. Depths range from 10-35 ft. Zone Two is suitable only for strong, confident ocean swimmers. Fins are recommended. On windy days or during periods of south swell, large incoming waves make swimming difficult and could wash you over the reef. Even under ordinary conditions, poor visibility often makes snorkeling unrewarding. On calm days, however, Zone Two is the best place to see living coral in shallow water. Fish life is abundant and even more diverse than in Zone One. A slight to moderately strong current running out through the channels can make the swim back in a bit tiring. The outgoing current is strongest in the middle of the channel.

Zone Three extends from Witch's Brew Point to the entrance of the bay. Again, this area is only for strong, confident ocean swimmers and is enjoyable only during calm weather. Depths range from about 20-70 ft. Visibility generally improves the farther out you go, but the waters in the center of the bay are too deep for surface snorkelers to see much. Fish abundance and diversity are highest along the sides of the bay, especially on the right side, although conditions there are often too choppy for comfort. Currents are possible beyond the mouth of the bay. If you are unsure of your abilities, speak to a lifeguard.

Walks. Broad ledges run along the left and right sides of the bay. When conditions are calm these ledges are open to visitors. (When the surf is up, however, the ledges can be dangerous. Large waves have knocked people down, bruising and lacerating them, or even washing them into the sea.) Walking along the left side of the bay leads around a point to the **Toilet Bowl,** a small, deep, active pool at the end of a narrow inlet. Connected to the inlet by a small tunnel, the pool alternately fills and empties with the waves. Snorkeling in this area is not recommended, but there are interesting geological formations and daredevils enjoy jumping into the pool. There are hazards here. The rock surrounding the pool can be extremely slippery and falls are common. Also, the sudden filling and "flushing" can be frightening to those who jump in unprepared. Some find it difficult to get out and panic. Others are thrown against the pool's sides by the violent inrush of water. If in doubt, stay out. Above all, never attempt to swim through the small narrow passage connecting the pool with the ocean.

The ledge along the right side of the bay leads to a rocky point called **Witch's Brew Point**. Beyond the point is a rough and choppy part of the bay called the **Witch's Brew**. The name is appropriate: floating debris often accumulates here, including old boards, nets, trash and other unappealing items. The beach side of the point, by contrast, is an excellent snorkeling area full of fish and live coral. It's possible to jump in off the ledge and snorkel, but there is no obvious and easy way to climb back out. It's better to snorkel in from the beach and return the same way.

The Toilet Bowl, a pool that fills and empties with the waves through a narrow subterranean tunnel, is a popular destination for those who walk the ledge on the left side of the bay. The surrounding rock can be extremely slippery, however, and accidents are common. BE VERY CAREFUL. There is no snorkeling here.

Sandman's Patch

Swimming Area

Channel

Witch's Brew

Ⓑ

Ⓔ

Ⓐ

Ⓓ

Keyhole Lagoon

Toilet Bowl

Ⓕ

Ⓒ

Channel

Back Door Lagoon

Details

Zone One details: Zone One, more commonly called "inside the reef," is where almost everyone snorkels. The entire area is protected and safe for swimmers. (Non-swimmers should confine themselves to wading next to the beach.) The Hawaiian word **kīpuka** means, among other things, a deep place in a reef, and in Zone One there are several beautiful **kīpuka**. In this book we call them lagoons, but the Hawaiian word is more accurate. Most prominent are the Keyhole Lagoon and the Back Door Lagoon, both at the left (northeast) end of the beach. As you walk down the road to the water you can look right down on them. These sandy-bottomed breaks in the reef are the most popular snorkeling areas in the bay and offer a good diversity of species. Here you will find fishes that live over sand (such as Striped Mullets and Threadfins), fishes that live over rock (such as Convict Tangs and Stocky Hawkfish), and fishes that hide under ledges or in rocky

Snorkeling inside the reef (Zone One). The tide is high and snorkelers can float over the top of the reef. A few people are visible in Zone Two, beyond the reef. Witch's Brew Point is in the background. It is an unusually calm day with no waves breaking.

crevices (such as Peacock Groupers or Hawaiian Cleaner Wrasses). In the slightly turbulent areas closest to the breaking waves you will see Achilles Tangs, Yellow Tangs, and other species that mostly dwell outside the reef. The lagoons are especially good areas in which to look for invertebrate animals such as sea cucumbers and colonies of living coral. Zone One is an excellent place to learn to identify Hawaiian corals because the colonies are isolated, easy to pick out, and easy to compare with one another.

In the rubble- and sand-bottomed "swimming area" fronting the center of the beach (created by blasting in the 1950s) you can find Flowery Flounders, Lagoon Triggerfish, Bandtail Goatfish, Snowflake Morays, and Barred Jacks. It's a great place to see some fishes that are pretty rare everywhere else, such as Bonefish and Hawaiian Ladyfish. Sometimes an octopus or two may be found here. The deep natural pool or

Striped Mullets schooling in the Back Door Lagoon, inside the reef (Zone One). Hanauma Bay is a great place to see species such as these that are rare or fished out most everywhere else.

Green Turtles often enter the inner reef area (Zone One) to graze on algae. This one in Sandman's Patch has come to the surface to breathe.

A small Undulated Moray hunts in the rubble- and sand-bottomed Swimming Area.

A Bluefin Trevally joins it, hoping to nab some animal scared out of hiding by the eel. Hunting associations like this are common at Hanauma Bay.

kīpuka to the right of the Telephone Cable Channel is called Sandman's Patch. Originally larger, it was partially filled in when the telephone cables were installed. Sandman's Patch is a good place to look for Green Turtles, Bluestripe Snappers, dense schools of Convict Tangs, Brick Soldierfish, Trumpetfish, and nesting Hawaiian Sergeants.

When the tide is moderate to high it is possible to float over the top of the reef from one deep area to another, but at low tide you will have to walk, wade, or swim the long way around. Park management requests that you do not climb up on the reef, sit on it, or walk on it. (If you do, someone will politely communicate with you over the loudspeaker system.)

Much of the water from waves breaking over the reef exits through the Telephone Cable Channel (also called the Slot), creating a slight counterclockwise current in the swimming area in front of the beach. This slight current makes it easier to swim from the left end of the beach toward the center than the from the center to the left, but the effect is minor. The channel itself is a different matter. The current here often exerts a definite pull into Zone Two. If you are not a strong, confident ocean swimmer, stay out of the channel. The same goes for the Back Door, a poorly defined exit at the far end of the Back Door Lagoon.

Zone Two details: Comparatively few snorkelers at Hanauma venture beyond the inner reef; conditions outside are often too rough and visibility too poor for enjoyable snorkeling. If you are comfortable and confident in the ocean, however, there are two ways into Zone Two. The easiest and most obvious is through the Telephone Cable Channel (also called the Slot) approximately in front of the lifeguard tower at the center of the beach. The channel lies immediately to the right of a line of dark boulders, visible except during the highest tides. The second way out is through the somewhat obscure passage called the Back Door, located at the far end of the Back Door Lagoon at

A Hawaiian Cleaner Wrasse picks parasites off a large parrotfish at its cleaning station in Sandman's Patch.

Orangespine Unicornfish are common inside the reef (Zone One), often in pairs. Thoroughly used to people, they can be approached closely. Note the sharp orange spines at the base of the tail fin.

Two Threadfin Butterflyfish probe for small organisms in the sandy floor of the Back Door Lagoon.

A male Hawaiian Sergeant guards its nest of purplish eggs in Sandman's Patch. Breeding males often display a metallic bluish color to attract females and to warn off other intruding males.

Sailfin Tangs, named for their extendable dorsal and anal fins, are common inside the reef. When alarmed they spread their fins, appearing instantly to double in size.

A large Bluefin Trevally patrols the top of the Boulder Reef. Often one individual in a pair, perhaps the male, turns almost black. Large jacks like these are common in Hanauma Bay but have been fished out most everywhere else.

the left end of the beach. Water from waves washing over the reef exits through both of these channels and unless the tide is high there is usually a slight to moderately strong outgoing current. Swimming out is fast and easy. Getting back in may be a bit of a slog. It's best to wear fins if you explore beyond the reef and to go only when the sea is calm.

The easiest and closest snorkeling area outside the reef is along the face of the fringing reef (area A on the aerial photo). If you exit through the Telephone Cable Channel, swim to your left along the front of the boulders and beyond. If you exit through the Back Door, swim to your right. Along the face of the reef at depths of 5-15 ft. you may see schools of Yellowfin Goatfish, sticklike Trumpetfish, exotic Moorish Idols, large Bluefin Trevallies, a school of Bigeye Trevallies, Teardrop, Raccoon and Longnose Butterflyfish, and many others. There is much more marine life outside the reef than in. Coral is sparse in front of the boulders because the reef here was destroyed during the laying of the first trans-Pacific telephone cable in 1956, but visibility is often better than in nearby areas and there are often more fish.

A second good snorkeling area with plenty of live coral lies between the Telephone Cable Channel and Witch's Brew Point (area B). (The Witch's Brew itself, a rough, choppy part of the bay where floating debris accumulates, lies seaward of Witch's Brew Point.) Perhaps the best single spot in area B is on the inner, or beach, side of the point. The water here is often clearer than in surrounding areas, and there are typically more fish. Venture here only when the water is calm. Because it is far from the beach, some people walk out along the ledge and jump in, but there is no particularly easy place to climb in and out. Most snorkelers swim out from the Telephone Cable Channel, follow the twin cables for a bit, then cut over to the right toward the point. Much of the

Convict Tangs often browse the reef in large schools, thereby overwhelming the defenses of territorial herbivores such as the Brown Surgeonfish, the Pacific Gregory, and the Achilles Tang.

With long snouts, bold colors, and graceful trailing filaments, Moorish Idols are classic coral reef fish. This pair was photographed in the Witch's Brew area.

Bigeye Trevallies in the Witch's Brew area. These predators, like many others, rest by day in schools and disperse at night to feed.

bottom to the right of the cables is covered with massive mounds of yellow-brown or greenish Lobe Coral. This is a true living reef. The fossil reef in Zone One probably resembled this 3,000 years ago when sea level was six feet higher. Notice the occasional deep, sandy-bottomed holes (**kīpuka**). Plenty of fish live throughout this area. You will see Hawaiian Cleaner Wrasses servicing their "customers," Spectacled Parrotfish scraping at coral, pretty Oval Butterflyfish, bizarre Scrawled Filefish and many more. Sightings of octopuses and turtles are common.

A third snorkeling area lies toward the left side of the bay (**area C**) where the bottom consists largely of coral heads interspersed with sand. This beautiful part of the bay is not often visited. Expect depths of 10-20 ft.

Finally, right in the center of the bay and just inside Zone Two is a small section of reef covered with Cauliflower Coral that rises to within about 6 ft. of the surface (**area D**). The sand patch from which it rises is about 15 ft. deep.

Zone Three details: This area is for strong, experienced ocean swimmers only and is recommended only during periods of light winds and small seas. Wear fins. Lobe Coral, dominant in Zone Two, gradually gives way here to Finger Coral, which prefers depths of about 30 ft. or more. Much of the bottom in Zone Three is too deep for snorkelers to enjoy unless the

Early-morning snorkelers have the best chance of seeing interesting and unusual behaviors, such as this Milletseed Butterflyfish picking parasites from a group of Sharpnose Mullets in Sandman's Patch.

Black Triggerfish and Hawaiian Sergeants are superabundant in parts of Zones Two and Three, chiefly along the right side of the bay where they feed in midwater on plankton.

water is very clear. Deep sand channels separate the reefs. The sides of the bay are shallower, however, and home to greater numbers of fish. Beyond Witch's Brew Point on the right side, the bottom is covered with huge blocks and boulders that create ample shelter for marine life (**area E**). As a result, this area probably hosts a higher concentration of fishes than any other part of the bay. Snorkelers will see impressive aggregations of Hawaiian Sergeants and Black Triggerfish feeding on plankton high in the water, and perhaps a mixed swarm of Yellow Tangs and other surgeonfishes grazing on the bottom below. Expect schools of Yellowfin Goatfish and Raccoon Butterflyfish as well. Unfortunately, this side of the bay receives the easterly tradewind swell and is normally too choppy and stirred up for enjoyable snorkeling.

Milletseed Butterflyfish attacking the egg patch of a Hawaiian Sergeant. The defending male has no chance against such a swarm.

Surgeonfishes near Pai'olu'olu Point, far out in Zone Three. It has to be flat calm to venture safely this far out in the bay. This area is for experts only.

For experts only, further out toward the right-hand entrance to the bay expect schools of Milletseed, Pennant, and Pyramid Butterflyfishes, Whitebar Surgeonfish, and Gray Chubs. Depths range from 15-50 ft. You are far from the lifeguards here, and no one will be able to see you. Unless seas are exceptionally calm, turbulence along shore can be extreme. A slight to moderate current sometimes moves across the entrance to the bay, usually to the right, so be mindful of where you are. As long as you stay well inside the bay the risk from currents is low. (See p.42.)

The left side of the bay in Zone Three (**area F**) is more sheltered in normal tradewind weather than the right, thus visibility is often better. The best snorkeling is along the shore where in places the rocky sides are thickly covered by compact heads of branching Cauliflower Coral. This beautiful area is rarely visited—you will probably have it to yourself. Depths are 15-20 ft. Area F is more or less continuous with area C in Zone Two.

Unless the water is unusually clear, the Finger Coral reefs in Zone Three are too deep for surface snorkelers to see much detail. The tops of these reefs typically lie at about 35-45 ft. and their bases at about 50-60 ft. One of the Finger Coral reefs near the Witch's Brew, however, is of particular interest. Turtles have long used it as a resting place and have flattened the coral in numerous places to make "beds" for themselves. If the water is clear, you might spot several turtles lying motionless far down on the reef below. If you are lucky, you might see surgeonfishes cleaning the algae off the turtles' backs. If by chance you are capable of diving that deep, keep your distance and do not disturb the resting turtles. For that matter, never pursue swimming turtles or attempt to make contact with them. Turtles are protected by federal and state law.

Equipment

You can rent masks, snorkels, and fins at the concession stand, but for the best fit and most comfortable experience it is best to bring your own. Ideally, you will have all three pieces. If you have just bought a mask and are using it for the first time, you should know that brand-new masks tend to fog up during use unless the lenses are scrubbed. Toothpaste is the best agent to use. The mild abrasive in most brands is ideal for removing a substance that causes fogging, deposited on the glass during manufacturing. After the initial scrub, a little bit of baby shampoo rubbed on the lens and rinsed out will keep the mask clear, or you can buy antifog solutions made just for the purpose. Many people find that saliva does a good job too.

Best Time to Snorkel

Hanauma Bay is somewhat sheltered and can be enjoyed throughout the year. The bay opens to the southeast, however, and thus receives both easterly swells generated by the normal tradewinds and occasional storm-generated swells from the south. (The storms don't have to be local. Winter storms as far south as New Zealand and Antarctica can seriously affect summer snorkeling in Hanauma Bay!)

The very **best** time for snorkeling in the bay is when winds are light and there is little surf. This combination can occur at any time but is most likely from October to April, with January and February often particularly good. Late August and early September can favorable also. You can mitigate the effects of wind and surf by snorkeling at low tide and/or in the early morning. At low tide fewer waves wash across the reef and visibility is better, at least on the inside (Zone One). In the early morning the wind and waves tend to be at their minimum for the day. Also, other people have not yet stirred up the water.

The **worst** times to visit Hanauma Bay are: 1) On the day of the week that the park is closed—currently Tuesday. (Because changes are possible at any time, call the recorded information line at **396-4229** for the latest information.) 2) During periods of big surf from the south or when strong and gusty easterly tradewinds generate big surf from the east. This can happen at any time, but is most likely from May through September. Although the inner area generally remains protected and safe, waves washing across the reef at these times stir up the bottom and greatly reduce visibility. Snorkeling outside the reef during periods of big surf is likely to be completely unrewarding and, for the inexperienced, possibly dangerous. During periods of even moderate surf, park authorities usually close the Toilet Bowl and Witch's Brew ledges. 3) Another potentially bad time to visit Hanauma occurs seven to ten days after a full moon when box jellyfish sometimes come inshore to breed. When the box jellies come in, park personnel usually close the beach for the day. Luckily, this doesn't happen often. For an advisory on possible emergency conditions call the Hanauma Bay Nature Preserve recorded information line at **396-4229.**

Temperatures range from an average in the low 70s Fahrenheit (low 20s Celsius) during January and February to an average in the low 80s (high 20s Celcius) during September and October.

Tides in Hawai'i vary less than three feet. Zone One tends to be clearest at low tide, especially if it occurs in the early morning. For tide information call the Surf Report at 596-7873. The tide at Hanauma Bay is approximately one hour earlier than at Honolulu Harbor. Be aware that some high tides are not very high (e.g., 0.4 ft.) and some low tides are not very low (e.g., 0.6 ft.). If you need detailed information look at a tide calendar, available in bookstores and fishing supply shops. O'ahu tide charts are also posted on the internet. As the tides change, mild to strong tidal currents run parallel to the coast in many areas. The inside of Hanauma Bay, however, is free of dangerous currents.[1]

Forecasts and information: For wind, tide, and surf conditions at selected O'ahu beaches call the Surf Report at **596-7873** (596-SURF). Hanauma Bay is not mentioned in these reports, but the conditions at nearby Sandy Beach are likely to be similar. Reports are updated at 7 AM, noon, 3 PM, and 7 PM. If the surf at Sandy Beach is "one to two feet," conditions at Hanauma are probably excellent. If "one to three feet," they are normal. If "two to four feet," they are marginal. If higher, forget it. If the Surf Report line is constantly busy (a sign of high surf somewhere on O'ahu!), call the City and County of Honolulu Ocean Safety and Lifeguard Services Division at **922-3888**. Press ext. 3 for current ocean and beach conditions. This report is not updated as frequently as the Surf Report. Another line to try is the National Weather Service at **973-4383**. The National Weather Service also does not update its reports as frequently as the Surf Report, and it uses a different system for measuring wave height. The National Weather Service reports "true wave height" which basically doubles the "local wave height" figures given on the Surf Report. True wave height is the height of the breaking wave's face as seen from the beach. Local surfers measure wave height from behind the breaking waves. An excellent website for surf information is http://uhslc.soest.hawaii.edu/HILO/surfforc.html. Wave heights are given in both "true" and "local" scales.

Note that the Hanauma Bay Nature Preserve recorded information line **(396-4229)** does not usually give weather or surf conditions.

---

[1] Much has been written about a current called the "Moloka'i Express," reported by some guidebooks to sweep unwary snorkelers out to sea from inside the bay. This is myth. Although the current is real, it does not occur in Hanauma Bay. According to Clark's *Beaches of O'ahu* the true Molokai Express sweeps around Portlock Point in the vicinity of Koko Kai Beach Park on the opposite side of Koko Head from Hanauma. It can come up suddenly at certain times of year, flowing opposite to the normal westerly currents, and has caught divers and surfers by surprise, pulling them along the Koko Head cliffs in the general direction of Moloka'i. The current that runs across the mouth of Hanauma Bay, however, is little different from the tidal currents that run parallel to shore along much of O'ahu's coastline, especially at times of a big tidal change. It usually pulls mildly from left to right, although reversals can occur. Currents intensify around points of land. It is best to stay well away from Palea and Pai'olu'olu Points at the far left and right sides of the bay.

SCUBA DIVING IN HANAUMA BAY

Although this book is primarily a snorkeling guide, some basic information for scuba divers is not out of place. The underwater map, in fact, was created mainly for divers. Make a color photocopy, laminate it, and take it with you. You will find it useful. Here are some diving tips followed by short descriptions of Hanauma's three easiest dives.

• Boats are prohibited in Hanauma Bay; all diving is from shore. At present, regulations do not require the use of dive flags in the bay because the waters are not legally navigable. (Almost everywhere else in Hawai'i you must dive with a flag.)

• Visibility is typically poor close to shore. The farther out you go, the better it gets, but do not expect more than about 50-60 feet. Maximum depths inside the bay are about 70 feet.

• During infrequent periods of light winds and calm seas, dive charters operating out of Hawai'i Kai sometimes take boats to locations just outside the bay. Visibility here can be 100 feet on a good day. If you are interested in this inquire at dive shops. Such dives, however, are seldom scheduled; the waters outside the bay are generally too rough for boat diving.

• To avoid standing in line with your heavy dive gear on, lock it in your car and go through the line first. After paying the entrance fee, ask to get your hand stamped, then return to your car and gear up. On your way down to the beach show your stamped hand to the guard. He or she will let you through.

• The tram will carry you and your dive gear down to the beach for the normal fee plus an extra charge for the gear. You can walk down and ride back up, or walk both ways if you are in good physical condition. The road is steep, however, and heavy exertion immediately after diving increases susceptibility to decompression sickness; if you aren't in good aerobic condition bring money with you and take the tram back up.

• To identify all the fishes seen while diving you will need a more complete fish book than this one; it was compiled primarily for snorkelers.

Here are Hanauma Bay's three easiest dives. Others dives are possible, but these will get you started. Remember: no matter where you dive in the bay, you can safely surface and swim back to the beach. That's the advantage of no boat traffic.

DIVE 1: THE CABLES

Enter the water in front of the lifeguard tower at the center of the beach and swim out through the shallow Telephone Cable Channel (also called the Slot). Look for two old undersea communication cables that emerge from the bottom just beyond the wave-break zone. Submerge at any point and follow the cables out to the Finger Coral reefs at center of the bay and beyond.

Because visibility generally improves in the center of the bay, many divers prefer to swim out on the surface as far as Witch's Brew Point or beyond before submerging. After exploring the reefs, follow the cable back the way you came. This is the easiest and most popular dive in the bay. The cables make navigation easy.

DIVE 2: THE BACK DOOR

Enter at the Back Door Lagoon at the far left end of the beach. Swim out through the shallow Back Door Channel and beyond. Dive along the left side of the bay and/or explore the long Finger Coral reef that parallels it. If you have enough air, explore the area in front of Toilet Bowl Cove before turning around.

You can return the way you came, but finding the Back Door Channel from outside the reef can be tricky. Consider using the map to navigate over to the twin cables, then follow them in through the Telephone Cable Channel. You'll end up conveniently near the restrooms and showers.

DIVE 3: WITCH'S BREW

If Witch's Brew Ledge is open, walk out almost to the point and find a place to climb or jump in on the beach side of the point. (There is no single good place to enter and exit.) Swim out beyond the point and submerge. Head toward the entrance of the bay. As you get farther out the bottom becomes strewn with large boulders creating a habitat for masses of fish. You can explore this area and/or use the map to find the cable that runs around Pai'olu'olu Point. Follow the cable as long as air permits, then return to Witch's Brew Point and climb out, or follow the cable back in to the beach. Another possibility is to swim on the surface out toward the entrance of the bay, then descend. This maximizes your time in the deeper, clearer water near Pai'olu'olu point. Here the cable runs over some enormous boulders and there are lots of fish. Follow the cable back or return the way you came. Diving this far out in the bay is for the experienced only and best done with a guide. Some currents are possible at the entrance to the bay.

SAFETY TIP:

Diving from the beach requires swimming through one of the two channels that lead outside the reef. A surprisingly strong outgoing current flows through them, particularly at low tide. Although it's easy to swim out, it can be difficult to get back in with cumbersome dive gear on. It may be easiest to swim in under water, even though the depth is only a few feet. Be sure to save some air for this. If you are unsure of your capabilities speak with a lifeguard. More rescues are made in these channels than in any other part of the bay.

CONSERVATION AND REGULATIONS

The marine environment, particularly around coral reefs, is under stress throughout the world. Overfishing, blast fishing, pollution, siltation, coastal development, and other assaults linked to a rising world population are rapidly taking their toll. Hawai'i's shores are just as vulnerable as those elsewhere. What can an individual do to help?

A good way to begin is to learn and respect the laws regarding the taking of marine life. Hawai'i has good laws but many residents remain unaware of them, or take a relaxed attitude toward them.

Even better, know and respect marine life itself. Do not take anything from the sea that you do not truly need. For most of us, this means taking nothing, even where permitted.

Also, minimize your impact on the marine environment. Almost everything in the sea harbors life—even rubble and sand. Know this and be gentle.

Finally, support the creation of more marine preserves like Hanauma Bay. They are desperately needed.

Activities prohibited in Hanauma Bay
The Division of Aquatic Resources of the State of Hawai'i Dept. of Land and Natural Resources has prohibited the following activities in the Hanauma Bay Marine Life Conservation District (MLCD):

- Fishing for, taking, or injuring any marine life (including eggs), or possessing any device that may be used for the taking of marine life. (However, it is permitted to possess a knife in the water for personal safety.)

- Taking or altering any sand, coral, or other geological feature or specimen, or possessing in the water any equipment that may be used for taking or altering a geological feature or specimen.

- Introducing any food or other substance into the water to feed or attract marine life.

- Operating any watercraft.

The Hanauma Bay park management requests that you do not sit, stand, or walk on top of the reef. Algae, small organisms, and colonies of coral live on its surface. Damage caused by one person might be undetectable, but the cumulative effect of thousands of visitors over a period of years could be significant. For the same reason, learn to recognize living coral and avoid handling or grabbing it.

Also, federal and state laws prohibit harassing marine mammals and turtles. Marine mammals seldom enter the snorkeling areas, but if you see a turtle make no attempt to pursue it or to make contact with it. (Turtles generally ignore snorkelers who float quietly in their vicinity, and this is perfectly acceptable.) Similarly, please do not chase fish, pick up sea cucumbers, or make deliberate contact with other forms of marine life. Let the creatures be.

Mahalo.

WHAT IS A FISH?

Surprisingly, there is no precise answer. Originally, "fish" meant any animal that spends its entire life in the water. (It is still used that way in the words "jellyfish," "starfish," "cuttlefish," etc.). Today, however, when we say "fish" we usually mean any of several types of aquatic animals that have gills throughout life, a backbone of some sort, and (generally) a streamlined body with fins.

This is probably as good a place as any to mention that the plural of "fish" depends on use—scientists prefer "fishes" when referring specifically to multiple species but "fish" when referring to members of a single species or when species is unimportant. Thus we can correctly say that there are over 20,000 species of **fishes** in the world, thousands of **fish** in a school, and billions of **fish** in the sea.

Scientists that study fishes are called ichthyologists. Through study of fossils, ichthyologists have determined that we are in a golden age of fishes. There are probably as many or more species living today than at any time in the Earth's past! And more are being discovered every year.

Fish are important. They are the oldest and largest group of vertebrate animals—accounting for slightly more than half of the total species—and are ancestral to all others. Scientists believe that the terrestrial vertebrates reptiles, birds, and mammals—descended from fish that evolved to live on land. (Curiously, some of these land animals returned to the sea millions of years later to become our present-day sea turtles, sea snakes, seals, dolphins, and whales.) Not only are fish the most diverse and species-rich of the vertebrates, they are also, perhaps surprisingly, among the easiest to observe.

Striped Mullet

FISH ANATOMY

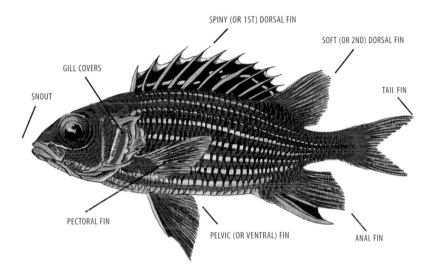

SPINY (OR 1ST) DORSAL FIN

SOFT (OR 2ND) DORSAL FIN

GILL COVERS

TAIL FIN

SNOUT

PECTORAL FIN

PELVIC (OR VENTRAL) FIN

ANAL FIN

Ichthyologists usually work from preserved specimens and perform their identifications in the laboratory, typically by counting fin spines, scale rows, teeth, and the like, and by examining the structure of other parts such as the gills. For the purposes of this book, such refinements are not necessary. The shapes, sizes, and color patterns of live fishes are usually enough for identification in the field.

It is difficult, however, to describe the characteristics and colors of fishes without elementary knowledge of fish anatomy. One must at the very least know the names and locations of the principle fins, such as the dorsal or pectoral fins. For this purpose a self-explanatory diagram is included. Wherever possible, common rather than scientific words are used, i.e. "tail fin" for "caudal fin" and "base of tail" rather than "caudal peduncle." Another distinction is useful: "stripes" are horizontal while "bars" are vertical.

CLASSIFICATION AND NAMES

Planet Earth has more than 20,000 fish species. They are classified into a hierarchy of evolutionarily related groups known as **classes, orders, families,** and **genera**. Genera are then separated into individual species.

The **class** is the broadest grouping. Of the four classes of living fishes, only two are of interest here: the ancient cartilaginous fishes (sharks, rays, skates, and chimaeras) and the more modern bony fishes.

The **order**, one level down, is a grouping of broadly similar fishes. All eels, for example, belong to the order Anguilliformes. Most reef fishes belong to the perchlike Perciformes. Other examples of orders are scorpionfishes (Scorpaeniformes) and tubemouthed fishes such as pipefishes, seahorses, trumpetfishes, and cornetfishes (Syngnathiformes). Note that the names of orders usually end in "...iformes." There are 29 orders of living fishes, of which the perchlike Perciformes is by far the largest.

Families are composed of closely related fishes within an order for example, moray eels (Muraenidae) and goatfishes (Mullidae). The names of families always end in "...idae." This book is organized alphabetically by the common names of families.

Within families are even more closely related groups known as **genera** (singular: **genus**). Finally, each genus is divided into **species**. (Specialists may also divide one species into two or more subspecies.)

The formal, scientific names of fishes consist of two parts: the genus and the species. This "binomial nomenclature," invented by the great Swedish naturalist Carolus Linnaeus (1707-1778), is used in the naming of all animals and plants. In print, the genus is always capitalized while the species is entirely in lower case, as in *Chaetodon auriga*. Both are italicized.

Binomial names are often, but not always, composed of descriptive Latin or Greek words. *Chaetodon*, meaning "hair tooth," is a genus within the butterflyfish family Chaetodontidae. (The first syllable rhymes with "key.") The species name *auriga*, meaning "charioteer," indicates precisely which butterflyfish we mean, in this case, the Threadfin Butterflyfish, *Chaetodon auriga*, named for the whiplike filament trailing from the dorsal fin.

It has often happened (especially in the last century) that two or more scientists, working in different parts of the world, each "discovered" and named a fish of the same species. Confusion has resulted, with some fish receiving a dozen or more published scientific names. The rules of scientific nomenclature state that, within certain limits, only the first published name for a species is valid. Later names are known as "synonyms." Great progress has been made in recent years toward sorting out synonyms and valid names. That work is still going on, and some of the scientific names in this book will undoubtedly be revised in the future. Similarly, older books may use a scientific name different than the one given here.

Scientific names can be intimidating to nonscientists. They look difficult and hard to pronounce, and they frequently do not connect in any obvious way with the actual plant or animal. Nevertheless, if one wants to communicate precisely about plants and animals, scientific names have no substitute. This book tries to make the scientific names more meaningful by providing translations whenever practical.

Common or popular names present another dilemma. A single fish species can have half a dozen popular names, varying from country to country or even region to region within a country. In some parts of the United States, but not Hawai'i, scientists have attempted to standardize the English names of fishes, as has been done for birds and molluscs. This is a worthy goal, although it sometimes results in names which few people actually use. This book attempts to solve the problem by giving alternate common names wherever practical.

In the Hawaiian language, fish names are rich and detailed. Fishing was an important part of life in old Hawai'i, with many connections to other activities. Different varieties of sugar cane, taro, or sweet potato, for example, often shared names with fishes. The Hawaiians had as many as four or five different names for a single fish species, designating different stages of its growth. Sometimes fish names had parallel meanings important in ceremony and magic.

Hawaiian fish and plant names were often in two parts, a general name coupled with a specific descriptor (similar to the genus and species of a scientific name). Thus **humuhumu** (triggerfish) and **'ele'ele** (black) join to form **humuhumu 'ele'ele**, the Black Triggerfish or Black Durgon *(Melichthys niger)*. Unfortunately, by the time anyone thought to record Hawaiian fishing lore much of the old culture and knowledge had been lost. In many cases only the general name has survived. Although secondary descriptive names have been recorded, we often do not know exactly to which species they refer. Many Hawaiian names remain in common use, especially for the more important food fishes. Translations have been provided wherever practical.

FISHES BY FAMILY

Angelfishes (Pomacanthidae)

Snorkelers are unlikely to encounter angelfishes in Hanauma Bay, but how can a fish book not mention these most popular of fishes? Small, quick moving and shy, they live along the deeper slopes of the reef under ledges, in thickets of coral, or in rubble—all places where snorkelers cannot see. Furthermore, they seldom stay still for long, a flash of color revealing them as they dart from one hiding place to the next. Their often bright colors may serve to warn away competitors, and to predators the colors may say: "Remember me. I'm hard to catch and not worth the effort." Of the approximately 80 angelfish species worldwide, 5 occur in the main Hawaiian Islands. Four are endemic, and none have Hawaiian names. A single common species is described here.

POTTER'S ANGELFISH • *Centropyge potteri* •

The only truly common angelfish in Hawai'i, these are rusty orange darkening to black with vertical gray-blue bars and blue trim on the fins. Males have more blue. They generally live in small groups under ledges or in thickets of coral at depths of 15 ft. or more. Occasionally they occur in shallower water, but snorkelers would be extremely lucky to see one. Divers, of course, see them frequently. In Hanauma Bay they occur only outside the reef. They feed on algae. The name honors Frederick A. Potter, director of the Waikiki Aquarium from 1903-1940. To 5 in. Endemic to Hawai'i. Photo: Magic Island, O'ahu.

Barracudas (Sphyraenidae)

Lean, fast, and powerful, barracudas have reputations as predators second only to sharks. They are elongated and almost cylindrical in cross section, with a pointed, protruding lower jaw, two dorsal fins spaced widely apart, and a large forked tail. The mouth, often held slightly agape, is full of sharp teeth.

The reputations of dangerous marine predators rise and fall. Sharks, for example, were downplayed in the early 1900s when many scientists thought them stupid and cowardly. At the same time barracudas were widely regarded as fearless and liable to strike without warning. One authority even claimed that barracudas were responsible for most "shark" attacks. Today the pendulum has swung to the other side: sharks are treated with respect and caution, while barracudas are seldom considered a threat.

Barracuda attacks, although rare, can cause serious injury. Generally they occur in murky water when a barracuda mistakes the flash of jewelry on the victim's hand for a silvery fish. There have been no recorded attacks in Hanauma Bay, where barracudas are typically wary of humans and seldom large. If you see one it will likely swim away faster than you can swim after it. At least two species of barracudas occur in Hawaiian waters. Only the Great Barracuda, below, is likely to be seen by snorkelers.

GREAT BARRACUDA • **kākū** • *Sphyraena barracuda*

The largest of the barracudas, this species is silvery, often with small black blotches irregularly placed on the lower side. The large tail fin is black except for the tips, which are pale. Smaller specimens may have about 20 indistinct bars. They occur alone or in groups of two or three and usually swim in midwater or near the surface. In Hanauma Bay they often enter fairly shallow water just outside the reef and occasionally enter the lagoons as well. Early morning is the best time to see one. If the water is clear enough for you to identify the barracuda, the fish should also be able to identify you and there is no reason to be alarmed. Attacks are very rare and tend to occur only when visibility is greatly reduced. Great Barracudas attain a length of 6 ft. with a weight of about 100 pounds, but those in Hanauma Bay are generally 2-3 ft. long. The species occurs in warm waters worldwide. The common name originates from South America. Photo: Witch's Brew.

Blennies (Blenniidae)

Blennies are small, elongated fishes typically seen in tide pools or peering from holes in the reef. Their alert eyes, doleful expressions, and curious antenna-like filaments (cirri) make them favorite close-up subjects of underwater photographers. They also make entertaining and comical aquarium pets and, for marine biologists, interesting subjects of study.

Blennies may be divided into two broad categories: bottom-dwellers and free swimmers. The former subsist mostly on algae and organic deposits (detritus) scraped from the rocks with their wide mouths. They are poor swimmers, lack air bladders, and sink as soon as they stop moving. When out of their holes they prefer to rest on rock or coral.

The free-swimming fang blennies are carnivorous, swim openly, and retreat to their holes only at night or when threatened. Their lower jaws bear a set of curved fangs used primarily for defense. If taken by a larger fish, a fang blenny will bite the inside of its captor's mouth and be spat out unharmed. In some non-Hawaiian species the fangs are venomous. These venomous species are often mimicked by yet other blennies!

Many fang blennies feed exclusively on mucus or bits of scale scraped or nipped from the sides of larger fishes. These tiny predators make sneak attacks on their larger hosts, sometimes relying on mimicry to approach within striking distance. For example, one color form of the Ewa Fang Blenny, a Hawaiian blenny not illustrated here, sometimes resembles juveniles of the Hawaiian Cleaner Wrasse.

With over 300 species, the blennies form a large family. The ancient Greeks knew them as *blennos,* the source of our modern name. The general Hawaiian name is **pāoʻo**. Of the 14 blennies known from Hawaiʻi, the four below are most easily seen while snorkeling in Hanauma Bay. Not shown is the shy Scarface Blenny (black with red markings on the face), which also inhabits the inner reef area. Because of this family's short larval stage, many Hawaiian species are endemic.

BULLETHEAD BLENNY • **pāo'o** • *Blenniella gibbifrons*
[BULLETHEAD ROCKSKIPPER]

These blennies are common on shallow, wave-washed reef flats in just a few inches of water. At Hanauma Bay, look for them peering from their holes right at the top of the fringing reef. Light greenish-brown, mottled and barred with darker brown, they blend well with the substrate. Males have blue-white spots on the sides and sometimes blue throats (perhaps breeding coloration); females have red spots on the head. The leading edge of the first dorsal fin of both sexes bears a dark spot. There is no crest. The eyes and forehead bulge out slightly, conferring both common and species names (the latter meaning "humped front"). To about 5 in. Indo-Pacific. Photos: near Sandman's Patch.

Bullethead Blenny—male breeding coloration

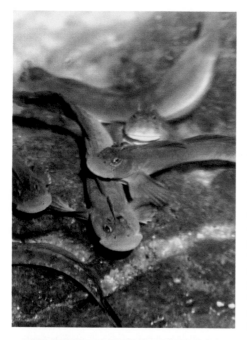

ZEBRA BLENNY • pāoʻo • *Istiblennius zebra* ●
[Jumping Jack, Rockskipper]

Anyone who pokes about Hawaiʻi's rocky shores is familiar with these fish. At Hanauma Bay look for them around the edges of the bay as you walk to the Toilet Bowl or the Witch's Brew area. They live in calm pools above the high tide line, never in the ocean itself, and feed exclusively on organic matter (detritus) that accumulates on the rocks. They swim with side-to-side undulations like little eels or bask in the sun along the sides of their pools, almost out of the water. When alarmed (they can spot a potential land predator 50 ft. away) they can leap, slither, and skip a surprising distance over the rocks, somehow knowing in advance the location of the next pool. Their color varies from a smart blue-black to brownish gray with indistinct bars, hence the name. A crest and two tentacles (longer in males) adorn the head, but collapse entirely when out of the water. Large territorial males develop yellowish white cheek patches. To 7 in. Endemic. Photo: Makapuʻu, Oʻahu, in splash pool.

GOSLINE'S FANG BLENNY • *Plagiotremus goslinei* ●
[Scale-Eating Blenny]

This free-swimming fang blenny is mostly black or gray on the back with a whitish to light blue stripe along the center of the body. It feeds on the scales, skin, and mucus of larger fishes; its mouth, underslung like that of a tiny shark, contains two long fangs used only for defense. Snorkelers are sometimes nipped by these little fish (usually on the leg) but they do no harm. If chased, the blenny usually backs tail first into an abandoned worm hole, leaving only its head sticking out. At Hanauma this species is most common outside the reef, occasionally inside. The name honors ichthyologist William A. Gosline, for many years a professor at the University of Hawaiʻi. To 2 1/2 in. Endemic. The similar and more colorful Ewa Fang Blenny *(P. ewaensis),* most likely to be seen outside the reef, is black to orange, usually with iridescent blue body-length stripes.

Boxfishes (Ostraciidae)

Spotted Boxfish (male)

Boxfishes are completely encased in rigid armor plate; only their fins, eyes, and mouths are movable. Sometimes called trunkfishes, they are immediately recognizable by their shape, usually square in cross-section, but sometimes triangular, pentagonal, hexagonal, or even round. Like pufferfishes, to which they are related, boxfishes rely in part on poison to deter predators. When they are disturbed their skin secretes a toxin. Captured boxfishes, kept in a small container, can poison themselves as well as any other fishes held with them. The poison (ostracitoxin) is not known to affect humans. Boxfishes eat algae, sponges, tunicates, worms, and other invertebrates found on the sea bottom. In many species, adult males and females are differently patterned, males being more colorful. Immature fishes of both sexes, however, share the "female" pattern. This explains why small boxfishes with male coloration are never seen.

Observed up close, boxfishes are definitely "cute." It is always fun to watch them scull about in their boxlike shells, with their little mouths per petually puckered, as if to kiss. Although they appear slow, they can move surprisingly fast and can easily outswim a snorkeler. Boxfishes belong to the order Tetraodontiformes, which includes such other odd creatures as porcu-pinefishes and triggerfishes. Their family name comes from the Greek *ostrakon* ("shell" or "potsherd"). In old Hawai'i they were known in general as **pahu** ("box" or "drum"). Of five species occurring regularly in Hawai'i, the following is most likely to be seen by snorkelers.

Spotted Boxfish (male)

Spotted Boxfish (female or immature male)

SPOTTED BOXFISH • **moa** • *Ostracion meleagris*

Females and immature males are black, densely covered with white spots. Mature males have dark blue sides with black spots and markings; their tops are black with white spots; their heads and tails are adorned with gold trim. Everywhere but in Hawai'i males have gold spots on the sides. Usually lacking these, the Hawaiian population is regarded as the subspecies *camurum* (although males with scattered gold spots on their sides are occasionally seen). Spotted Boxfish often forage in the shallows where the water is calm and may be seen by waders as well as by pedestrians walking along the edge of the bay. Snorkelers can find them in deeper water too. These fish are solitary; it is unusual to see two together unless they are preparing to spawn. The species name means "guineafowl" (a bird native to Africa covered with light spots). Indo-Pacific and Eastern Pacific. To about 6 in. Photos: Back Door Lagoon. See also p.17

Butterflyfishes (Chaetodontidae)

If there were a typical coral reef fish, it would probably be a butterflyfish. Brightly colored (often in yellow), pairs of these delicate creatures are a common sight as they flit among the undersea gardens. Their disklike bodies, like artists' palettes, display colors and patterns obviously meant to be noticed.

While most other fishes have evolved to blend with their environment, the butterflyfishes have done the opposite. What advantage do they gain? They are spiny and make a prickly mouthful—is their appearance a warning? They travel in pairs and may mate for life—is it for recognition? Whatever the reason, if there is a reason, these fishes delight and inspire all visitors to their undersea realm.

With their disk-shape bodies, butterflyfishes are well suited for maneuvering through narrow spaces. Though they might seem easy targets for predators, they can quickly move out of reach. To further confuse their foes, most species have a dark bar through the eye, effectively disguising it. Some go one step further, displaying a false eyespot near the tail. Depending on the species, butterflyfishes feed on small invertebrates, plankton, coral polyps, and occasionally algae, often using their snouts to probe into crevices. Although they have long-term, possibly permanent mates, butterflyfishes release their eggs into the water (as do most fishes) and offer no care to their young; after hatching, the larvae drift with the plankton for weeks or months.

In old Hawai'i, butterflyfishes had several general names. Those called **kīkākapu** ("strongly prohibited") are described in several chants as sacred. Others were **lauhau** ("leaf of the **hau** tree") or **lauwiliwili** ("leaf of the **wiliwili** tree"). There were specific names as well, but it is no longer clear to which species they referred.

Anatomically, butterflyfishes are characterized by small, brush-like teeth. The family name, Chaetodontidae, is a combination of *chaeto* ("hair") and dentis ("tooth"), the first syllable rhyming with "key." Of the approximately 115 butterflyfish species, 22 occur in the Hawaiian Islands and 13 are pictured here. Hanauma Bay is a great place to see butterflyfishes.

THREADFIN BUTTERFLYFISH • kīkākapu • *Chaetodon auriga*

These butterflyfish swim in pairs and are common inside the reef at Hanauma Bay, often feeding over sand or rubble bottoms. Their whitish body darkens to gold in back and is marked with sets of fine right-angled diagonal lines. One of the soft dorsal spines is prolonged into a threadlike filament; below it is a black spot. Like many of their family members, Threadfin Butterflyfish pairs defend territories within which they roam freely. Other butterflyfish species are tolerated but those of the same species are driven away. The species name means "charioteer," probably because of the whiplike dorsal filament. To about 8 in. Indo-Pacific. Photo: Back Door Lagoon.

SADDLEBACK BUTTERFLYFISH • kīkākapu • *Chaetodon ephippium*

Among the most striking of their family, these fish are gray with a bold black saddle rimmed in white. They have an orange snout and a dorsal filament similar to that of the Threadfin Butterflyfish. Uncommon in Hawai'i, they almost always occur in pairs and roam widely within a large home range. They can be found both in shallow turbid water inside the reef and in clear deep water outside. A pair has lived in the Back Door Lagoon and surrounding areas for many years. Reef fishes, including butterflyfishes, can live a surprisingly long time. A Saddleback survived in the Nancy Aquarium in France for over 25 years! To 8 in. Western and Central Pacific. Photo: Swimming Area.

BLUESTRIPE BUTTERFLYFISH · kīkākapu · *Chaetodon fremblii* •

Found only in Hawai'i, this attractive fish is yellow with eight narrow blue stripes running diagonally along the body. When alarmed it becomes a darker, dirty yellow. Individuals are common in shallow water, especially around patches of sand or smooth bottom between boulders and coral. These fish live in small groups consisting of a male and several females, an unusual arrangement for species of this family. Hawaiian endemics usually have close relatives elsewhere, but nothing like this fish is known in the entire Indo-Pacific. Species such as this are called "relicts" because all others of their lineage appear to have died out (or have changed beyond recognition). To 6 in. Endemic to Hawai'i. Photo: Back Door Lagoon.

LINED BUTTERFLYFISH · kīkakapu · *Chaetodon lineolatus*

As large as dinner plates, these striking fish usually occur in areas of rich coral growth, almost always in pairs. The numerous dark, vertical lines on the whitish body are distinctive. A dark bar completely hiding the eye is mirrored by a dark arc at the rear of the body. The dorsal, anal, and tail fins are yellow. Uncommon and difficult to approach, these wary fish are infrequently encountered in Hanauma Bay, usually along the right side beyond the Witch's Brew area. Occasionally a pair turns up in the Sandman's Patch area inside the reef. They grow to 12 in. and are the largest members of the butterflyfish family. Indo-Pacific. Photo: beyond Witch's Brew (Zone Three).

RACCOON BUTTERFLYFISH • **kīkākapu** • *Chaetodon lunula*

The face of this fish, with its masked eyes and white crescent-shape mark resembles that of its namesake, the nocturnal American mammal. The body, orange-yellow with diagonal brown stripes, darkens to brownish on the upper sides. A broad dark bar running diagonally back behind the eye is bordered in bright yellow, as is a dark spot at the base of the tail. Juveniles, which occur in tide pools (and sometimes inside the reef at Hanauma), are brighter yellow with a large false eyespot. In the early morning, schools of Raccoon Butterflies roam the reef feeding on fish eggs or whatever else they can find. Later in the day they often rest motionless in midwater, sometimes in aggregations that frequent the same locations year after year. At Hanauma, schools usually occur outside the reef. Inside, these fish are typically found singly or in pairs. The species name means "crescent." To 8 in. Indo-Pacific. Photo: Reef Face area (Zone Two).

MILLETSEED BUTTERFLYFISH • **lauwiliwili** • *Chaetodon miliaris* •   ➡
[LEMON BUTTERFLYFISH]

Yellow with vertical lines of dark spots, these are Hawai'i's most abundant butterflyfish (although they are not necessarily common in all locations). They feed mostly on plankton but will eat almost anything. When the opportunity arises, they descend in a great yellow swarm upon the purplish egg patches of the Hawaiian Sergeant, totally overwhelming the defending parent. Sometimes they will "clean" other fish by removing parasites. In areas where they have been hand fed they will mob snorkelers and divers, but even in pristine locations schools of these curious fish will approach humans in the water. Submarine observations show them to be the most common species at depths of about 150-300 ft. At Hanauma Bay they occur both inside and outside the reef but are most numerous in Zone Three, where large schools occur near the entrance to the bay on the right side. Smaller schools may also be seen in the Witch's Brew area. The Frenchmen who named these fish thought their spots resembled seeds of millet. To 6 1/2 in. Endemic to Hawai'i. Photo: Back Door Lagoon. See also p. 39

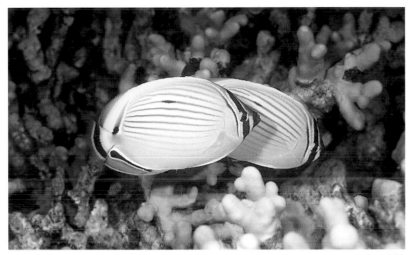

Oval Butterflyfish

OVAL BUTTERFLYFISH • **kapuhili** • *Chaetodon lunulatus*
[REDFIN BUTTERFLYFISH; MELON BUTTERFLYFISH]

These exquisite and richly colored fish are apricot gold, set off with purple gray lines and tinges of red on the anal fins. Their scarcity along most Hawaiian reefs only enhances the delight of finding them. Like many other butterflyfishes, they almost always occur in pairs and probably mate for life. At Hanauma Bay look for these fish outside the reef near coral, upon which they feed exclusively. Occasionally they show up inside the reef as well. This is one of the few butterflyfishes with a specific Hawaiian name—a word that also means "person with many taboos." Perhaps this fish was considered especially sacred. To 5 1/2 in. Western and Central Pacific. (An Indian Ocean butterflyfish, C. *trifasciatus*, is very similar. Until recently the two were considered to be the same species.) Photo: Finger Coral reef (Zone Three).

Milletseed Butterflyfish (see previous page)

MULTIBAND BUTTERFLYFISH •
kīkākapu · *Chaetodon multicinctus*

These small sedate butterflies are common throughout the Islands, probing and picking at the corals upon which they feed. Almost always tightly paired, they are light tan covered with brown dots, which coalesce to form four or five vertical bars. Coral-eating butterflyfishes such as these take only a few nibbles from a colony and then move on, thus minimizing damage to their food source. They defend a feeding territory from which they drive other coral-eating butterflyfishes. In Hanauma Bay this species lives only outside the reef, usually around Cauliflower Coral, its preferred food. The species name means "many bands." To 4 in. Endemic to Hawai'i. Photo: Lāna'i Lookout, O'ahu.

ORNATE BUTTERFLYFISH · **kīkākapu** · *Chaetodon ornatissimus*

Among the most beautiful of butterflyfishes, these are cream color with black bars on the face and graceful orange lines running diagonally along the body. Most of the body is rimmed in black. At Hanauma they occur both inside and outside the reef, but they are more common outside. They feed exclusively on living coral and, like most coral-eating butterflyfishes, occur in mated pairs. If you see one, a second is usually nearby. To 8 in. Indo-Pacific. Photo: Reef Face area (Zone Two).

FOURSPOT BUTTERFLYFISH • **lauhau**
Chaetodon quadrimaculatus

Despite both the common and scientific names, only two white spots are visible on these fish. (To make four, the spots on both sides must be counted.) Their bodies are dark brownish black above, becoming orange-yellow below, with a yellow tail and a yellow head and the usual dark stripe through the eye. At Hanauma Bay they occur both inside and outside the reef. In most locations in Hawai'i they subsist largely on polyps of Cauliflower Coral *(Pocillopora meandrina)*, but where there is little of this, as inside the reef at Hanauma, they eat algae and small invertebrates. To 6 in. Known only from the islands of the Pacific. Photo: Palea Point (Zone Three).

TEARDROP BUTTERFLYFISH • **lauhau** • *Chaetodon unimaculatus*

This lovely yellow and white butterflyfish is immediately recognizable by the large black upside-down "teardrop" on the side. In larger specimens the downward-pointing lower part fades, leaving a round black spot. Its large blunt mouth, unusual for a butterflyfish, is capable of nipping off bits of the hard encrusting corals upon which it feeds. These fish occur singly, in pairs, or in small groups. In Hanauma Bay, snorkelers outside the reef will almost surely see a few. Occasionally they venture inside the reef as well. The species name means "one spot." To about 8 in. but usually smaller. Indonesia to Hawai'i. A similar species, *C. interruptus,* occurs in the Indian Ocean. Photo: Sandman's Patch.

LONGNOSE BUTTERFLYFISH • **lauwiliwili nukunuku ʻoiʻoi** • *Forcipiger flavissimus* [FORCEPSFISH]

Probably more than any other fish except the Moorish Idol, Longnose Butterflyfishes have come to symbolize the exotic beauty of the coral reef. Their long probing snouts, bristling dorsal spines, and intense yellow color are unmistakable. They frequent walls and ledges and often swim upside down on the roofs of caves. Of the two almost identical species of *Forcipiger* (the other, *F. longirostris,* is rare in Hanauma Bay), this has the shorter snout. (Some call it the Forcepsfish to differentiate it from its even longer-nosed cousin.) It is also the most widespread of all butterflyfishes, ranging from Mexico to the Red Sea. In Hanauma Bay look for it outside the reef, especially by the Boulder Reef at the left of the Telephone Cable Channel. It may be solitary, in pairs, or in threes. It has the longest of all Hawaiian fish names: **lauwiliwili** ("leaf of the **wiliwili** tree"), **nukunuku** ("beak") and **ʻoiʻoi** ("best" or "sharp"). The species name might be translated as "extreme yellow." To 7 in. Indo-Pacific and Eastern Pacific. Photo: Boulder Reef area (Zone Two).

PYRAMID BUTTERFLYFISH • *Hemitaurichthys polylepis*

This handsome schooling butterflyfish is found near steep drop-offs along current-swept points, preferring depths of 40 ft. or more. A solid white triangle rimmed with yellow marks the body; the head is dark brown. Large schools of these fish are almost always found at Paiʻoluʻolu Point at the entrance to the bay on the right-hand side. On rare calm days they sometimes move into the bay as far as the Witch's Brew area, where snorkelers can see them. They feed on plankton. The species name means "many scales." To 6 in. Western and Central Pacific. A similar species, H. *zoster,* occurs in the Indian Ocean. Photo: Mackenzie State Park, Hawaiʻi.

PENNANT BUTTERFLYFISH • *Heniochus diphreutes*
[Bannerfish; Pennantfish]

Immediately recognizable by their bright white pennants, these schooling plankton-eaters are boldly patterned with white and black vertical bars; their soft dorsal and tail fins are yellow. Rare specimens have a double pennant. These fish school along current-swept drop-offs, usually at depths of 40 ft. or more, but on rare occasions, usually during the summer, they enter the bay where snorkelers can see them. A school of Pennant Butterflyfish is one of the prettiest underwater sights in Hawai'i. Juveniles live near the bottom, often around isolated outcrops of coral. Don't confuse this fish with the Moorish Idol (p.138), which is similar although unrelated. To about 8 in. Indian Ocean, subtropical Western Pacific, and Hawai'i. Photo: Pai'olu'olu Point (Zone Three).

Sea Chubs (Kyphosidae)

Sea Chubs are heavy-looking, generally gray fishes with oval bodies, small pointed mouths, and large tails. Also called rudderfishes or **nenue**, they often school in shallow rocky areas where they feed on algae. In the days of sailing ships they would congregate around the rudders of ships in harbor, feeding on algae and perhaps wastes thrown overboard. The common Gray Chub loves handouts. Before fish feeding was banned in Hanauma Bay these fish would swarm around snorkelers and waders, sometimes becoming pushy and aggressive. In their eagerness they would sometimes bite a hand (though not maliciously), earning them the nickname "Hanauma Bay piranhas." Juvenile chubs often congregate under floating objects, far from land. This family of herbivores includes about 45 species worldwide. Three species occur in Hanauma Bay, both inside the reef and out. The differences between them are subtle. Most abundant is the Gray Chub. If you can learn to identify the other two as well, you are an expert fish watcher—give yourself a pat on the back!

Gray Chubs at Pai'olu'olu Point (Zone Three)

Typical coloration

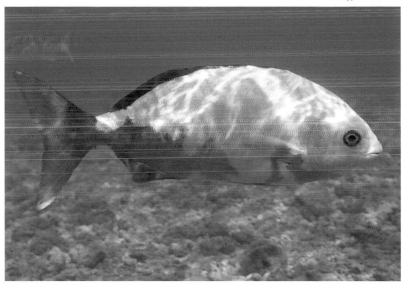

Multicolored individual

GRAY CHUB • **nenue** • Kyphosus bigibbus
[Brown Chub]

Hawai'i's most common chub, this fish is usually dull gray to silvery. Stripes following the scale rows are faint (compare with the Lowfin Chub, next page); a pale line often marks the curve of the back. Occasional individuals are bright yellow, orange, white, or multicolored. (In old Hawai'i a yellow or white chub was regarded as "queen" of the school.) Gray Chubs are abundant at many snorkeling and diving locations in Hawai'i, including Hanauma Bay and Molokini Islet, Maui. At Hanauma they were once abundant inside the reef, although this is not typical habitat for the species. Feeding over the years drew them in; they have become less numerous since feeding was banned. To 2 ft. Indo-Pacific. Photos: a) typical coloration; b) multicolored individual. Keyhole Lagoon.

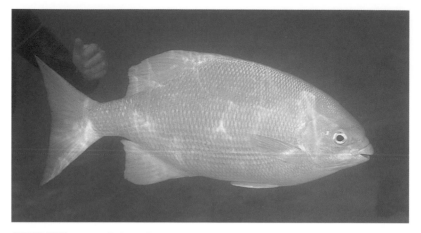

HIGHFIN CHUB • nenue • *Kyphosus cinerascens*
[SNUBNOSE CHUB]

High soft dorsal and anal fins and a snub nose give this chub a distinctive profile. The body may be light silvery gray as pictured here or blackish with light flecks. The scales are more prominent than in the two species above. At Hanauma Bay, Highfin Chubs are common along the outer face of the reef, and on top of the reef when the tide is high. One or two can usually be seen inside the reef as well. The species name means "ashy" or "ash color." To about 14 in. Indo-Pacific. Photo: Swimming Area.

LOWFIN CHUB • nenue • *Kyphosus vaigiensis*
[BRASSY CHUB]

These chubs have faint brassy yellow marks about the mouth, eyes, and at the edges of the gill covers (brighter in small individuals). The prominent scale rows create a slightly striped appearance, also helpful for identification. While these fish are grazing, evenly spaced pale round spots appear on their backs and sides; if threatened they darken their body, dramatically intensifying these spots. Lowfin Chubs also school, sometimes mixing with the more common Gray Chub. When snorkeling in Hanauma Bay, look for Lowfin Chubs near the turbulent surge zone or on top of the reef, where small individuals occur singly or in groups. The species name is from the Indonesian island of Waigeo. To about 20 in. Indo-Pacific. Photo: Swimming Area.

Damselfishes (Pomacentridae)

Damselfishes are small, often colorful fishes abundant in shallow, tropical habitats. A coral reef without them would seem empty. In Hawai'i, small fishes aggregating above coral heads are almost sure to be damsels. So are the small, drab, aggressive fishes common on reef flats or in the rocky shallows. The ubiquitous sergeants are members of this family, as are the striking clownfishes that inhabit and protect stinging sea anemones in other parts of the Indo-Pacific. Many damselfishes are brightly colored, while others are plain. Some are social, others are solitary. Few species exceed 6 in. and most are considerably smaller.

Although there are exceptions, damselfishes generally fall into two broad categories: plankton-eaters that feed in midwater and algae-eaters or omnivores that feed off the bottom. The former usually hover in groups above the reef, picking their minute prey from the water. The latter are typically solitary, inhabiting shallow, rocky areas where algal growth is heaviest and protecting their territory from competitors such as surgeonfishes or other damselfishes. Most algae-eaters feed also on small invertebrate animals and/or organic detritus.

The damselfishes form one of the largest fish families, with about 325 species. Seventeen occur in Hawai'i but few have Hawaiian names, probably because most are not important food fish. Hawai'i lacks the brilliantly colored damselfishes common elsewhere in the Pacific and Caribbean. The four species below are common at snorkeling depths in Hanauma Bay.

Hawaiian Sergeants at Palea Point (Zone Three)

HAWAIIAN SERGEANT • **mamo** • *Abudefduf abdominalis* •

This is one of the most common fishes in Hanauma Bay, both inside and outside the reef. The young, which are yellowish with five black bars, occur in tide pools. As they grow, the yellow fades to greenish white and the black bars shorten. Around the Witch's Brew area and beyond, Hawaiian Sergeants swarm high in the water to feed on plankton. When disturbed they dive as one for cover, but they soon rise again to resume feeding. In addition to plankton, they also consume algae or anything else they can find. Males commonly guard large purplish patches of eggs, laid by females on the walls of large crevices, on the sides of boulders, or on flat hard bottoms. They vigorously chase away all intruders. Occasionally, however, other fishes—including wrasses, butterflyfishes, and triggerfishes—overwhelm the defending parent. The resulting feeding frenzy may last several minutes or more, until the frantic male is able to repel the invaders. Sandman's Patch is a good place to see these fish nesting (see p.34). The Hawaiian name is from **ma'oma'o** ("green"). The name "sergeant" is shared by several Indo-Pacific and Atlantic species of the same genus and is probably American in origin—sergeants in the British Army wear a crown instead of stripes. To almost 10 in. Endemic to Hawai'i. Photo: Keyhole Lagoon. (See also p.16. This endemic's probable ancestor, the Indo-Pacific Sergeant *A. vaigiensis,* has recently established itself in Hawai'i. Juveniles of this species often aggregate under floating objects far from land; it may have arrived here with abandoned or lost fishing gear.)

Normal adult coloration

Courtship coloration

BLACKSPOT SERGEANT · **kūpīpī** · *Abudefduf sordidus*

This large, shallow-water damselfish varies from yellowish gray to dark brown with five to seven light bars. Males courting females or defending eggs become almost black, with highly contrasting white bars. A black spot on the upper base of the tail, always present, confers the common name. Juveniles and subadults, common in tide pools, have indistinct bars and a yellow wedgelike mark on the back. These damsels are omnivores, eating algae, crabs, sponges, molluscs, and anything else they can find. They are solitary, inhabiting areas of moderate surge around rocks and boulders, and are one of the most common fishes inside the reef at Hanauma Bay. The species name means "dirty," probably referring to its coloration. To about 9 in. Indo-Pacific. Photos: Sandman's Patch.

HAWAIIAN DASCYLLUS • 'ālo'ilo'i
Dascyllus albisella •
[Hawaiian Domino Damselfish]

Juveniles, jet black with a porcelain-white spot on each side and a neon-blue spot on the forehead, usually live in and around heads of branching coral. Adults leave the coral to live in loose aggregations, generally in deeper water. Adults lose the forehead spot. Their black bleaches out to grayish, and their white side spot becomes diffuse, sometimes expanding until the fish is almost entirely white. Snorkelers in Hanauma Bay occasionally find the perky little juveniles in heads of Cauliflower Coral, generally outside the reef. Adults typically live beyond the range of snorkelers at depths of 30 ft. or more. This endemic Hawaiian damselfish is closely related to the Domino Damselfish *(D. trimaculatus)* found elsewhere in the Indo-Pacific. The species name is from albus ("white"). The Hawaiian name means "bright and sparkling." To 5 in. Endemic to Hawai'i. Photo: juvenile. Pupukea Beach Park, O'ahu.

BRIGHT-EYE DAMSELFISH • *Plectroglyphidodon imparipennis*
These tiny grayish yellow damsels defend very small territories, usually in small depressions along the top of the reef in shallow water. Although bisected by a dark bar, their eyes nevertheless appear bright yellow-white. They feed almost entirely on small, bottom-dwelling invertebrates. To about 2 1/2 in. Indo-Pacific. Photo: Pūpūkea Beach Park, O'ahu.

PACIFIC GREGORY • *Stegastes fasciolatus*
[YELLOW-EYE DAMSELFISH]

This drab, blackish or brownish gray damselfish has bright yellow eyes and a patchy unkempt appearance because some scales are lighter than others. An algae eater, it is common on reefs where it boldly defends a small territory against competitors, darkening its yellow eyes when displaying aggression. If a swarm of algae-eating Convict Tangs invades its territory, however, there is little it can do except wait for them to move on. Like similar Indo-Pacific and Caribbean damsels, it probably "farms" its patch of filamentous algae by removing undesirable growths. It also eats small invertebrates living in its algal farm. This is one of the most abundant fishes in Hanauma Bay, both inside and outside the reef. To about 6 in. Indo-Pacific, but with a slightly different color pattern in Hawai'i. Photo: Back Door Lagoon.

Eels (Muraenidae and Congridae)

Eels are a specialized group of fishes adapted to life in crevices and holes. Their long, snakelike bodies typically lack scales and paired fins, which would only impair movement in narrow spaces. Eels form an entire order of fishes (Anguilliformes) containing many hundreds of species in about 16 families. Only moray eels (family Muraenidae) and conger eels (family Congridae), however, are likely to be seen by snorkelers in Hanauma Bay.

Morays are among the most easily observed members of the reef community. They peer from their holes and watch the underwater world go by, their thick, muscular bodies remaining securely hidden. Some morays open and close their mouths rhythmically, displaying needle-sharp teeth; their necks swell and pulse alarmingly with each gulp. To humans this appears menacing, but the eels are only pumping water over their gills—their way of breathing. In the early morning or late afternoon some morays emerge to hunt, undulating across the sand or twining and turning among the rocks and coral. Often a foraging eel is followed by a jack, goatfish, or grouper hoping to grab prey flushed from cover by the eel. Some morays will also enter tide pools or slither across wet rocks. The Peppered Moray, a Hanauma Bay resident not illustrated here, will even launch itself out of the water to grab rock-dwelling crabs. But for every moray seen, many more remain hidden; most spend almost all of their lives within the recesses of the reef.

Morays are perhaps best known for their sharp teeth and supposedly nasty dispositions. Writers, however, disagree on the danger they pose. Alarming eel stories are common in older books, but recent authors agree that almost all documented attacks occurred after the eel was hooked, speared, molested, or fed by divers. Left alone, eels pose little threat. It is foolish, however, to stick one's hands into crevices and holes that may contain eels. Even small morays can inflict considerable damage; their backward-pointing teeth make extrication of a hand or finger difficult. If you are bitten, don't jerk your hand back in alarm but wait for the eel to let go by itself—admittedly easier said than done!

In the Hawaiian language, eels in general are called **puhi**. Many secondary names are recorded but it is no longer always clear to which species they apply. In old Hawai'i some eels were relished as food and considered "choicer than wives." Others were revered as 'aumākua, the physical embodiment of certain family gods. Fierce warriors were sometimes compared to "sharp-toothed eels," and when trouble was brewing thoughts were said to "wiggle like an eel."

Moray eels are well represented in Hawai'i, with over 40 species. The 5 below are the ones most likely to be seen by snorkelers inside the reef at Hanauma Bay. A species of conger eel is also illustrated. If you find an eel, treat it with respect and do not attempt to play with it. To protect beachgoers, the Dept. of Land and Natural Resources has made a practice of trapping and removing morays from the inner reef area of Hanauma Bay.

SNOWFLAKE MORAY • puhi kāpā • *Echidna nebulosa*

These attractive eels are whitish with black speckles and several indistinct rows of irregular dark blotches that usually have white or yellowish centers, producing a sort of tie-dyed effect. They are seen more often in rubbly areas than around coral. Snowflake Eels do not have sharp teeth, possessing instead pebblelike plates used for crushing the shells of crabs or other invertebrates. They often forage during the day and may be followed by a small jack or goatfish hoping to nab prey items missed by the eel. These eels occur both inside and outside the reef at Hanauma but are not common. The best place to look for one is in the Swimming Area. The species name means "misty" or "cloudy." The Hawaiian word **kāpā** means "to press or squeeze." To almost 30 in. Indo-Pacific and Eastern Pacific. Photo: Makaha, O'ahu.

STOUT MORAY • puhi • *Gymnothorax eurostus*
This smallish moray is highly variable in color, ranging from brown, covered with irregular light spots and marks, to white with a few dark spots and marks. In its darker form it could be confused with the Whitemouth Moray (next page) but lacks the bright white inner mouth. This is probably the most abundant shallow-water moray in Hawai'i, although it generally remains hidden from view. The species name means "stout," or "strong." To almost 2 ft. Indo-Pacific and Eastern Pacific, but only in cool subtropical waters. Photo: Back Door Lagoon.

YELLOWMARGIN MORAY •
puhi paka
Gymnothorax flavimarginatus
These large eels are finely mottled in yellow and brown, with a dark blotch over the gill opening. The tail tip is edged in yellow-green, giving them their common and scientific names. This is one of Hawai'i's largest morays, and also one of the boldest. The Hawaiian name means "fierce eel" and Hawaiians of old were very careful where **puhi paka** was concerned. If you find one, maintain a respectful distance. This eel is most common outside the reef but occurs inside as well. It sometimes forages in the open during the day and may be followed by large hungry jacks hoping to get a piece of the action. The species name means "yellow margin." To about 4 ft. Indo-Pacific and Eastern Pacific. Photo: Back Door Lagoon.

WHITEMOUTH MORAY · **puhi ʻōniʻo**
Gymnothorax meleagris

This, the most commonly seen moray in Hawaiʻi, is brown, covered with white dots. The inner mouth is entirely bright white. Eels of this species occasionally hold their white mouths wide open, possibly in a threat display, making for easy identification. Active by day they sometimes hunt openly on the reef, especially in the early morning, moving from coral head to coral head in search of fish and crustaceans. Sometimes predators such as jacks or goatfishes follow them to snatch up prey animals flushed from cover. In Hanauma Bay these eels occur both inside and outside the reef. The species name means "guineafowl" (an African bird covered with small white spots) or "spotted." The Hawaiian name means "spotted eel." To 3 1/2 ft. Indo-Pacific. Photo: Back Door Lagoon.

Whitemouth Moray hunting near Witch's Brew (Zone Three)

UNDULATED MORAY · puhi lau milo · *Gymnothorax undulatus*
This moray has narrow jaws full of long sharp teeth, including a row down the center of the mouth. The top of its head sometimes has a greenish yellow tinge. The body varies from dark brown with light speckles and irregular vertical lines or netlike markings, to the reverse—almost white with irregular brown blotches. It occurs from scuba-diving depths to shoreline waters only a few inches deep. Although most active at night, it also forages during the day. This is one of the commonest Indo-Pacific morays, and also one of the nastiest; do not attempt to play with it. In old Hawai'i it was relished as food. The Hawaiian name means "leaf of the **milo** tree." To 3 1/2 ft. Indo-Pacific and Eastern Pacific. Photo: Sandman's Patch area. See also p.31

MUSTACHE CONGER · puhi ūhā · *Conger cinereus*
[White Eel]
These large eels are plain brownish gray by day but when hunting at night they develop broad dark bars. A fold of skin along the mouth resembles a mustache. During the day they hide in crevices and holes. Careless, they often leave the tip of their bladelike tail sticking out. Because they differ slightly from others of their species, Mustache Congers in Hawai'i have been given the subspecies name *marginatus.* Congers do not have sharp teeth. The species name means "ash color." To about almost 4 ft. Photo: Back Door Lagoon.

Filefishes (Monacanthidae)

Closely allied to the triggerfishes, filefishes have narrow, compressed bodies and a long, stout dorsal spine that they raise when alarmed. Many rely on camouflage for protection and are able to change color quickly to match their surroundings. The popular name comes from the rough texture of their skin. The Hawaiian name, 'ō'ili ("sprout" or "come up"), probably refers to their frequently raised dorsal spine. Like triggerfishes, filefishes move by rippling their soft dorsal and anal fins and can swim backward or forward with equal ease. They lack pelvic fins entirely. In general, these fishes are omnivores.

Filefishes belong to the order Tetraodontiformes, which besides triggerfishes includes other odd reef fishes such as boxfishes and puffers. Of the seven species found in Hawai'i, the two below are most likely to be seen by snorkelers in Hanauma Bay.

SCRAWLED FILEFISH · **loulu** · *Aluterus scriptus*
[SCRIBBLED FILEFISH]

Thin as a board, covered with short blue lines like scribblings, and with a tail fin fully a third or more the length of its body, this is one of those fishes often called "bizarre." Its hairlike dorsal spine is scarcely visible even when raised, and the body can rapidly darken to a mottled camouflage pattern. Scrawled Filefish occur in the open ocean as well as close to shore. They eat jellyfish, zoanthids (colonial anemones), fire corals (which don't occur in Hawai'i), and other noxious or poisonous animals. In Hanauma Bay they will enter quite shallow water but tend to occur only outside the reef. The Hawaiian name refers to a group of endemic, greenish white fan-palms *(Pritchardia sp.)* similar in color to the fish. **Lou** means "to hook," and the fish was used in sorcery to cause death. The species name means "written upon." To over 3 ft. All warm seas. Photo: Molokini Islet, Maui.

BARRED FILEFISH • 'o'ili • *Cantherhines dumerilii*
These large, deep-bodied filefish are brownish gray with faint vertical bars on the side. A tuft of orange spines (longer in males) sprouts at the base of the tail, also orange. Equipped with powerful jaws and strong teeth, they can sometimes be heard crunching rock and coral, much like parrotfishes. They often travel in pairs, warily tilting their backs toward snorkelers as they swim. In Hanauma Bay, look for them both inside and outside the reef. The species name honors French naturalist Auguste Duméril (1812-1870). To about 15 in. Indo-Pacific and Eastern Pacific. Photo: Sandman's Patch.

Hawaiian Flagtails (see next page)

Flagtails (Kuhliidae)

Flagtails are a small family of silvery, perchlike fishes with a single dorsal fin. In many species the tail fin is banded, but in Hawai'i this coloration occurs only in juveniles. Nocturnal feeders, they rest during the day, either in caves or in areas of heavy surge. Known in Hawaiian as **āholehole**, flagtails have long been prized as food. According to an 1893 Hawaiian newspaper, when a chiefess in Hilo yearned for the "fat āholehole," runners brought them to her from Puna, still alive in their wrappings of seaweed. "Because the chiefess had a craving," it reported, "the distance was as nothing."

To the ancient Hawaiians, names were often significant on several levels. For example, the word **hole** means "to strip away" and the **āholehole** was prepared for eating by gripping the dorsal fin with the teeth and pulling the body away. These fishes were sometimes used in ceremonies for the "stripping away" of evil spirits. Early Caucasian settlers, with their white skins, were sometimes called **āhole** (not to be confused with **haole**, meaning "foreigner").

Of the two flagtail species in Hawai'i, the most common is shown below.

HAWAIIAN FLAGTAIL · **āholehole** · *Kuhlia xenura* •

These silvery, perchlike fish school tightly over the fringing reef at Hanauma Bay, often in moderately turbulent water. Near the Keyhole Lagoon, smaller ones congregate over sand in a foot or two of water where they can be seen easily by waders. At night these fish disperse to feed on plankton. Young **āholehole**, which have banded tails, are abundant in tide pools. They will enter brackish and even fresh water. In old Hawai'i only the young were called **āholehole**; adults were simply **āhole**. To 1 ft. Endemic to Hawai'i. For years this fish was known as *K. sandvicensis*. Photo: Boulder Reef (Zone 2).

Flatfishes (Bothidae and Soleidae)

Every habitat has its specialists, and flatfishes—flounders and soles—are masters of the sandy or gravelly seabed. Their greatly flattened, oval bodies lie almost flush with the bottom. Virtually invisible to predator or prey, they wait patiently for the small crustaceans or fishes on which they feed. Flatfishes begin life as normal fish, with eyes on either side of the head. As they grow, one eye actually migrates over the top of the head, eventually joining the other on the opposite side. During this process the fish starts leaning over, eventually ending up flat on the sand with the blind side down.

The underside of most flatfishes is white; the upper side is usually speckled or mottled to match the substrate. They are able to fine tune this pattern for almost perfect camouflage. To make doubly sure they are not seen, they can partially cover themselves with sand, the eyes protruding like little periscopes.

Flatfishes are so strange and different that they constitute their own order, the Pleuronectiformes. There are many species, including the enormous Barn-Door Halibut of northern seas, which can grow to 7 ft. in length and weigh hundreds of pounds. Of the seven flatfish families, only the left-eyed flounders (family Bothidae) are seen regularly inside the reef at Hanauma. Confident of their camouflage, they can often be closely approached. If disturbed, a flounder will take off rapidly in a cloud of sand. It typically swims ten feet or so in a straight line, lands, then flutters backward into the settling sand, which partially covers it. Thus the creature ends up well-hidden several feet from where you expect it. Small soles (family Soleidae) also occur in Hanauma Bay, although probably not inside the reef. They are nocturnal and seldom observed. The Hawaiian name for flatfishes is pākiʻi ("fallen flat" or "spread out").

Flowery Flounder

FLOWERY FLOUNDER · **pāki'i**· *Bothus mancus*
[PEACOCK FLOUNDER]

The largest and most commonly seen flatfish on Hawaiian reefs, the Flowery Flounder is pale to light brown with spots and blue flowerlike markings. It usually lies on hard substrate rather than sand. The eyed side has three unequal dark blotches in a row, the one nearest the tail smallest. The eyes of males are further apart than those of females, and males have a greatly elongated pectoral fin. The species name means "wounded" or "hurt." To 19 in. Indo-Pacific. The similar Panther Flounder (below) prefers sandy bottoms. Photo: Swimming Area, on large dead coral head.

PANTHER FLOUNDER · **pāki'i** · *Bothus pantherinus*

This flounder lives over sand and rubble, often well away from reefs, and is smaller than the species above. Sharp-eyed snorkelers in Hanauma Bay can sometimes spot them in the Swimming Area inside the reef, where they occasionally lie on the tops of smooth rocks as well as on sand. Their camouflage is superb and unless the fish moves it is not likely to be noticed. If you manage to spot one don't take your eye off it or you may never find it again! Males have an extended pectoral fin and more widely spaced eyes than females. To about 12 in. Indo-Pacific. Photo: Swimming Area.

Goatfishes (Mullidae)

Goatfishes are often among the first fishes seen by a snorkeler finning over the sandy bottom. They are easily recognized by their barbels, reminiscent of a goat's beard, with which they busily "taste" the sand for worms, molluscs, and other invertebrates. Some use their barbels to flush shrimps, crabs, or even small fish from crevices of the reef. When not feeding they tuck their barbels up out of sight. All goatfishes have a forked tail and two dorsal fins. Many can change color dramatically in seconds, and their resting colors may differ from their active colors. Variable, yet looking much alike, goatfishes are sometimes difficult to identify underwater. Most are bottom dwellers, but several of Hawai'i's most abundant species school in midwater during the day.

Despite the obvious similarity between members of the family, there is no general Hawaiian name for goatfishes. Some species, especially those with one or more body-length stripes, are known as **weke** ("to open") and were sometimes used in religious ceremonies when an "opening" or "releasing" was required. **Weke** under 7 in. are called 'oama. Other goatfishes are known as **moano**. Still others have individual names. All are prized as food. In the words of an old chant: "Delicious, delicious is the fish of the sea, the **moano** of the yellowish sea, delicious, delicious."

Goatfishes are sometimes called "surmullets," their family name coming from the Latin *mullus* ("mullet"). Ten native species inhabit Hawaiian waters; two are endemic (one from deep water). Six are shown here.

Yellowfin Goatfish often school in front of the Boulder Reef. When resting under ledges these fish usually turn reddish. (See next page.) Here they show their normal white and yellow color.

SQUARE-SPOT GOATFISH • weke'ā • *Mulloidichthys flavolineatus*
[WHITE GOATFISH; YELLOWSTRIPE GOATFISH]

This is the most common goatfish inside the reef at Hanauma Bay. It has a squarish black spot on the side embedded within a yellow stripe running from head to tail. The black spot, often intense while the fish is feeding, sometimes disappears. The body is whitish; the fins are whitish to yellowish. Square-Spot Goatfish sometimes occur in schools off the bottom, but inside the reef at Hanauma Bay are more likely to be seen foraging singly or resting in small groups on the sand or rubble. Unlike the species below, they never turn red. The Hawaiian name means "staring goatfish." To 16 in., but usually smaller. Indo-Pacific. Photo: Swimming Area.

YELLOWFIN GOATFISH • weke'ula • *Mulloidichthys vanicolensis*

Similar to the species above but lacking the black rectangular spot, these goatfish have yellow fins as well as a yellow stripe from eye to tail. The yellow stripe may be bordered faintly with blue. They feed only at night and rest during the day in tight schools, hanging motionlessly in midwater, usually at the same spot on the reef year after year. They also congregate in caves and under ledges, where they often turn entirely pink or red (including the yellow stripe and fins). When posing to be cleaned by Hawaiian Cleaner Wrasses they often adopt the darker red color, perhaps to make parasites stand out. In Hanauma Bay snorkelers can usually find these under ledges in Sandman's Patch (often with Brick Soldierfish) or along the front of the Boulder Reef. The Hawaiian name means "red goatfish." The species name is from Vanikoro in the Solomon Islands. To 15 in. Indo-Pacific. Photo: Sandman's Patch. See also previous page.

DOUBLEBAR GOATFISH • **munu** • *Parupeneus bifasciatus*
Two widely-separated dark bars (the first often narrower) give this fish its common and scientific names. The gray body can lose its dark bars, however, or become reddish overall, or have bluish tints, or display all three variations at the same time! The tail is usually dark with a thin, light blue margin. This solitary goatfish, deeper bodied than many others, can also be identified underwater by its rounded profile, thick lips, and the slightly rounded margins of its tail fin. It prefers shallow habitats where coral is sparse. At Hanauma Bay look for it both inside and outside the reef. To 13 in. Indo-Pacific. Photo: Swimming Area.

MANYBAR GOATFISH • **moano** • *Parupeneus multifasciatus*
A dark stripe through the eye and three unequal black bars on the rear half of the body distinguish this fish. The ground color may be whitish to reddish or some of each. The pelvic and anal fins are sometimes beautifully colored in shades of magenta and blue. This is one of Hanauma Bay's most common goatfishes both inside and outside the reef. The species name means "many bars." The Hawaiian name means "pale red." According to Hawaiian legends, **moano** were said to become red by eating the red blossoms of the **'ohi'a lehua** tree. To 11 in. Pacific Ocean. Photo: Swimming Area.

WHITESADDLE GOATFISH · kūmū · *Parupeneus porphyreus* •

This goatfish can be grayish purple, reddish, or greenish but almost always has a small white spot (or saddle) above the base of the tail. Light streaks along the body above and below the eye are another identifying feature. It used to be common, but since the introduction of the Bluestripe Snapper into Hawaiian waters its numbers have declined. Highly valued in ancient times, this fish had five different names depending on its stage of growth. It was sometimes used in offerings calling for a pig, when a pig was unobtainable, and was forbidden to women, as was pork. The similar word **kūmū** means master; when a student attained full mastery in any endeavor a **kūmū** was often offered. Juveniles sometimes occur in tide pools. The species name means "purple." The Hawaiian name was also used for a variety of red-stalked **kalo** (taro) and in modern times has come to mean "good-looking" or "handsome." To 15 in. Endemic to Hawai'i. Photo: Sandman's Patch.

BANDTAIL GOATFISH · weke pueo; weke pahulu · *Upeneus taeniopterus*
[NIGHTMARE WEKE]

These are the only native Hawaiian goatfish with a banded tail. Two stripes run the length of the body, one brown and one yellow. The barbels are pale to bright lemon yellow. These fish forage in tight schools along shallow sandy bottoms near the shoreline, typically followed by a small jack. Often they are seen in only inches of water. Inside the reef at Hanauma Bay is one of the few snorkeling spots in Hawai'i where they occur. The brain of this fish is sometimes toxic; if eaten it can cause disturbed sleep and hallucinations. In old Hawai'i offerings to Pahulu, King of Ghosts, were believed to prevent ill effects. For this reason the fish was sometimes called **weke pahulu**. The 5-6 tail bands on each lobe of the tail fin resemble the bands of the **pueo** or Hawaiian owl, hence the other Hawaiian name. (The similar Yellowbanded Goatfish, *U. vittatus,* an accidental introduction, has fewer [3-4] and thicker bands on the lower lobe of the tail fin.) Some books list this fish as *U. arge.* To about 12 in. Indo-Pacific. Photo: Swimming Area.

Gobies (Gobiidae)

Although snorkelers and divers in Hawai'i seldom notice them, gobies form by far the largest family of fishes, with approximately 1,900 described species worldwide. The typical goby is a small, blunt-headed, somewhat elongate fish, often dwelling in a burrow or hole—but gobies have adapted to many other habitats, including tide pools, exposed mudflats, and the surfaces of living corals. The pelvic fins of most gobies are fused into a single appendage resembling a suction cup with which they cling or perch. In general, they are omnivores. Bottom-dwelling species sift mouthfuls of sand for small animals, algae, or detritus. The free swimmers and some coral-dwelling gobies probably pick plankton from the water.

Gobies are known in Hawaiian as 'o'opu. In addition to the 'o'opu kai (marine gobies), there are four species of 'o'opu wai (freshwater gobies), two of them endemic. One, the remarkable mountain-climbing o'opu alamo'o *(Lentipes concolor),* scales the rocky sides of waterfalls to reach the headwaters above. Scientists have recently found it above 1,000-ft. Hi'ilawe Falls, Hawai'i's highest free-falling cascade located in the Big Island's Waipi'o Valley. Once abundant, freshwater gobies were highly regarded as food in old Hawai'i.

About 28 species of marine gobies are known in the Islands, a disproportionately small number compared with other areas of the Indo-Pacific. Many inhabit sandy or silty bottoms rarely explored by snorkelers and divers. Others are restricted to tide pools. Three species are illustrated here. The Greek word for goby, *kobios,* is the source of our modern name.

HALF-SPOTTED GOBY
Asterropteryx semipunctatus

These small gobies inhabit coral rubble in silty, well-protected lagoons, bays, and reef flats. They usually perch in front of small holes into which they quickly disappear when alarmed. At Hanauma, they are common in the Swimming Area inside the reef. Their dark gray bodies are peppered with tiny blue spots, especially on the lower half (thus both the common and species names). The first three dorsal spines are usually prolonged into filaments. Mature females have one to seven yellow spots on the base of the tail. To about 2 1/2 in., but usually smaller. Indo-Pacific. Photo: Kāne'ohe Bay, O'ahu. 2 ft.

COCOS FRILL GOBY • 'o'opu 'ohune • *Bathygobius cocosensis*

This goby is seen in tide pools around the rim of the bay. Its dark color blends well with Hawai'i's black volcanic rock, but it can lighten to match other backgrounds. White spots may pepper head, body, and fins. It might be mistaken for the abundant and active Zebra Blenny (p.54), which shares similar habitat. The species is named for Cocos Island in the Indian Ocean, where presumably it was first discovered. To about 3 in. Indo-Pacific. Photo: Witch's Brew Ledge.

EYEBAR GOBY • *Gnatholepis anjerensis*

These pale gobies live on sand and rubble bottoms at the bases of boulders or coral heads and in Hanauma along the sides of the pools and lagoons. They retreat into crevices when alarmed. Although common inside the reef, they blend with the sand making them difficult to see. The name refers to a dark line extending through the eye and down the side. (In South Africa they are called "weeper gobies.") Look for a small bright yellow spot above the pectoral fin base. Scattered dark and white specks mark the body, and a row of smudgy dark spots runs along the lower side. The species name is from Anjer, Indonesia, where the species was first collected. To about 3 in. Indo-Pacific. The Hawaiian Sand Goby *(Coryphopterus sp.),* a fish of similar size and habits, also occurs inside the reef at Hanauma. Photo: Keyhole Lagoon

HAWAIIAN SHRIMP GOBY• *Psilogobius mainlandi* •

This small goby lives on silty sand bottoms where it shares a burrow with either of two species of snapping shrimps. The nearly blind shrimp digs and maintains the hole, while the goby, with its keener senses, stands guard at the entrance. The shrimp, which labors underground clearing and extending passages, emerges at intervals pushing a load of rubble like a little bulldozer. When near the entrance it always keeps one antenna in contact with the goby's tail fin. At the slightest sign of danger, the goby twitches its tail signaling the shrimp to retreat. If danger is imminent, the goby follows. Sharp-eyed snorkelers inside the reef at Hanauma Bay can observe shrimp and goby pairs in the deeper areas of the two large lagoons. Although their holes are easy to spot (they enter the sand at an angle and have a pile of excavated sand in front), the occupants may not emerge if there are lots of swimmers about. Early morning is a good time to look for them. The burrows are under constant construction and may shift location from day to day. Occasionally these gobies live in empty burrows made by other animals, such as mantis shrimps. Many species of shrimp gobies are known; this is the only one from Hawai'i. The name honors zoologist Gordon Mainland who drew attention to this fish while a student at the University of Hawai'i. The goby attains about 2 1/2 in., the shrimps about 1 1/2 in. Both are usually smaller. The goby is endemic; the shrimps have Indo-Pacific distributions. Photos: Keyhole Lagoon.

A mated pair of Hawaiian Shrimp Gobies rest outside their hole in the Keyhole Lagoon. The female is swollen with eggs. A rival male looks on.

Groupers (Serranidae)

Groupers are heavy-bodied, large-mouthed, bottom-dwelling predators. Usually solitary, they occur from shallow water to depths of many hundreds of feet. Some grow to enormous size. They have a protruding lower jaw, and their tail fin is typically rounded. Most groupers are blotched, spotted, and dull, but a few are brightly colored. Many species are of commercial importance.

Groupers do not chase their prey but rely on ambush or careful stalking to get within striking distance. Some species follow foraging moray or snake eels in order to nab prey disturbed by the eel. A grouper's method of ingestion is common to that of many other fish predators, such as hawkfishes and scorpionfishes. When the prey animal is sufficiently close, the grouper snaps open its large expandable mouth. Water rushes in, carrying with it the grouper's meal. This operation takes only a fraction of a second and is surprisingly effective. The stomachs of large groupers have been found to contain lobsters, stingrays, porcupinefishes and sea turtles. At least one Indo-Pacific species, the Giant Grouper *(Epinephelus lanceolatus),* is capable of swallowing a man. Extremely rare in Hawai'i, it can weigh almost 900 pounds and attains a length of nine feet.

Although groupers and their relatives form one of the largest fish families, only one native grouper is common in Hawai'i, and it lives in deep water. The absence of shallow-water groupers—an important fishery resource in many parts of the world—prompted the State Division of Fish and Game in the 1950s to introduce three species from the South Pacific. Only one has survived to reproduce in Hawaiian waters. The word "grouper" (from the Brazilian Portuguese *garoupa*) is probably of Native American origin.

Adult coloration

PEACOCK GROUPER • **roi** • *Cephalopholis argus*

Introduced from Mo'orea, French Polynesia, in 1956, **roi** have become common throughout the Hawaiian Islands. Small individuals are dark brown and covered with fine iridescent blue spots. In larger specimens the spots fade somewhat and a series of light vertical bars may appear on the rear half of the body. The pectoral and tail fins are a lovely dark blue. These fish often sit on a coral head or at its base but quickly disappear into a crevice when approached. Inside the reef at Hanauma Bay, however, they are used to snorkelers and often allow a close approach. Snorkelers outside the reef may see one or two Peacock Groupers following a foraging Whitemouth Moray in hopes of snapping up small animals it might flush out. The species is named for the hundred staring eyes of the mythical monster, Argus. Because these fish are not native to Hawai'i, the Tahitian name, **roi**, has come into common use. To about 16 in. Indo-Pacific. Photos: Sandman's Patch.

Juvenile coloration

Hawkfishes (Cirrhitidae)

Hawkfishes are small to medium-size predators that spend most of their time perched motionless among rocks or coral branches. The pectoral fins, which help hold them in place, are typically thick and enlarged. Although not strong swimmers, hawkfishes are capable of descending swiftly on their prey and pursuing it vigorously for short distances. Characteristic of the family are curious tufts of filaments extending from the ends of the dorsal spines. Males maintain harems.

Of 35 species of hawkfishes worldwide, 6 are found in Hawai'i and 3 are described here. The Hawaiian name for most hawkfishes is **hilu piliko'a**, which means "coral clinging."

STOCKY HAWKFISH • **po'opa'a** • *Cirrhitus pinnulatus*

The Stocky Hawkfish blends in well with its environment and is easy to overlook. Preferring exposed rocky areas in shallow water, it wedges its pectoral fins into cracks to stabilize itself in the surge. Its robust, mottled body is blotched with blue, brown, and red and has three loose rows of white spots on the side. Hawaiian specimens have slightly more colorful markings on the head than their Indo-Pacific cousins. Known to fishermen as "rockfish," they are easily hooked but not greatly esteemed. In old Hawai'i it was said, "The fisherman who fools around in shallow water takes home a **po'opa'a**." The Hawaiian name means "hard head." Snorkelers in Hanauma Bay can see these both inside and outside the reef. To about 11 in. Indo-Pacific. Photo: Keyhole Lagoon.

BLACKSIDE HAWKFISH · **hilu pili koʻa** · *Paracirrhites forsteri*
[FRECKLED HAWKFISH]

The front half of this fish is brown, densely freckled in reddish black; the rear has a very broad black band bordered in white. Juveniles are half-white, half-black (divided lengthwise) and have a bright yellow back, looking somewhat like juvenile Saddle Wrasses. The species name honors the Forsters, father-and-son naturalists who accompanied Captain Cook on his second voyage to the Pacific and Indian oceans between 1772 and 1775. To almost 9 in. In Hanauma Bay, this fish is most common outside the reef. Indo-Pacific. Photo: Witch's Brew area (Zone Two) sitting on Lobe Coral.

ARC-EYE HAWKFISH · **pilikoʻa** · *Paracirrhites arcatus*

Although this hawkfish has two color patterns, the prominent "U" mark in back of the eye will always serve to identify it. The two patterns are: grayish brown to reddish with a broad white stripe on the side; and brown without the white stripe. This is one of the most common hawkfishes in Hawaiʻi. In Hanauma Bay look for it outside the reef in and around heads of branching Cauliflower Coral. To 5 1/2 in. Indo-Pacific. Photo: Palea Point (Zone Three).

Jacks (Carangidae)

The family Carangidae includes the jacks, trevallies, rainbow runners, leatherbacks, scads, and others. Most are swift, strong-swimming predators which frequent open water near drop-offs or over reefs. They are especially prized by fishermen for their spectacular fighting ability.

Jacks are typically silvery on the sides and undersides and bluish or greenish on the back. This color pattern, common among open ocean (pelagic) fishes, makes them difficult to see both from above and below. They have deep, narrow, streamlined bodies (varying in shape according to the genus) and deeply forked tails. In most species the base of the tail is slender and reinforced by specially strengthened scales called scutes.

Jacks and their relatives frequently patrol the reef in schools, although single individuals are not uncommon. In the early morning or late afternoon, hunting behavior intensifies as pairs or schools of jacks flash swiftly by, making sudden changes of direction to confuse or isolate their prey. Some species, however, rest by day and hunt at night. Jacks feed primarily on other fish, relying on superior speed to chase them down. They also forage on the bottom for crustaceans and other invertebrates. Occasionally a jack hovers near a feeding bonefish or goatfish, ready to dash in and snatch up any tidbits that may be uncovered. Jacks will also follow foraging eels for much the same reason. Not all jacks are predators. Some smaller members of the family, such as the scads, are schooling plankton-eaters.

There are about 140 species of jacks worldwide, with at least 24 known in Hawai'i. Hanauma Bay is one of the best places in the Islands to see jacks—they have been fished out most everywhere else. Most jacks are called **ulua** in Hawaiian. Juveniles are **pāpio**. The scientific family name comes from *caranga*, a Native American word.

BARRED JACK • **ulua** • *Carangoides ferdau*

Seven dark bars, sometimes faint, identify these jacks. Typically the body is bluish silver, often with tiny, scattered, black-centered gold spots on the upper sides. The pectorals may be yellow. Some individuals temporarily darken the entire body to almost black. Barred Jacks typically roam in small schools over sand or rubble bottoms adjacent to the reef. They feed on bottom-dwelling crustaceans and small fishes. Although the species is uncommon in Hawai'i, snorkelers can often see subadults in shallow water inside the reef at Hanauma Bay where they sometimes follow a feeding goatfish or bonefish to nab sand-dwelling organisms it may uncover. They also occur outside the reef. To about 21 in. Indo-Pacific. Photo: Swimming Area.

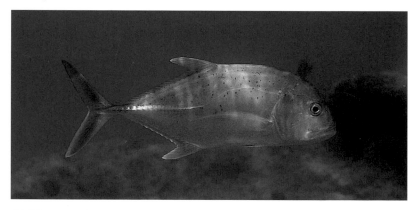

GIANT TREVALLY • **ulua aukea** • *Caranx ignobilis*
[WHITE ULUA; GIANT ULUA]

Known locally as White Ulua, these fish may be seen in pairs or as solitary individuals. In the Northwest Hawaiian Islands, where they are not heavily fished, they occur in large schools. They range from silvery to silvery gray, usually peppered with fine black spots. The steep profile of the head and a black spot at the base of the pectoral fin are identifying features. In Hanauma Bay juveniles and subadults are sometimes encountered inside the reef. Large adults are rarely seen anywhere around O'ahu. Although the biggest of its family, the species is inappropriately named "low" or "ignoble." The Hawaiian name means "white." In old Hawai'i when a human sacrifice was called for, a large **ulua aukea** was sometimes substituted. The species grows to over 5 ft. with a weight of almost 200 lbs. Indo-Pacific. Photo: Swimming Area.

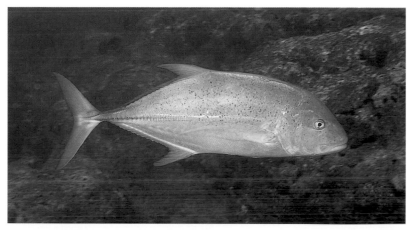

Normal coloration

Dark coloration

BLUEFIN TREVALLY • 'ōmilu • *Caranx melampygus*
[BLUE ULUA]

These jacks are silvery with scattered blue and black spots on the sides and lovely blue fins. They can quickly alter their color, however, becoming almost black. The most common large jacks in Hawai'i, they may be solitary, in pairs, or in small groups. At Hanauma Bay, subadults **(pāpio)** are common inside the reef, usually in small groups. Large adults often swim in as well, sometimes entering surprisingly shallow water. If you see small reef fish suddenly scatter and seek shelter, look over your shoulder—a pair of big Bluefin Trevally may be following you! To 39 in. Indo-Pacific and Eastern Pacific. Photos: Boulder Reef (Zone Two).

BIGEYE TREVALLY • **ulua** • *Caranx sexfasciatus*

Although rare in Hawai'i, these jacks are not uncommon in Hanauma Bay, where small schools often rest by day outside the boulder reef or in the Witch's Brew area. Sometimes they swim endlessly in a large circle. The upper edge of the gill cover has a black spot and the point of the second dorsal fin is white. Although they feed primarily at night, individuals may forage during the day in shallow water. The scientific name means "six-banded," but only **pāpio** (juveniles) display this pattern. They attain about 3 ft. but are seldom this size in Hanauma Bay. Indo-Pacific to Eastern Pacific. Photo: Boulder Reef area.

LEATHERBACK • **lai** • *Scomberoides lysan*
[QUEENFISH]

Leatherbacks, or queenfishes, have long, slender silvery bodies marked with a series of inconspicuous round spots. This species has a double row of 5-8 such spots, the lower larger than the upper. The dorsal fin is tipped with black. The skin is very tough and the spines are venomous. Years ago the skins of these fish were used for the heads of small drums; today they are used for making fishing lures. Solitary individuals and sometimes small groups of these fish are common in Hanauma Bay, usually swimming near the surface. Individuals often come inside the reef. To about 28 in. Indo-Pacific. Photo: Back Door Lagoon.

Ladyfishes and Bonefishes
(Elopidae and Albulidae)

Ladyfishes and bonefishes belong to the primitive order Elopiformes. Both are slender and silvery with a single dorsal fin and a deeply forked tail. They inhabit shallow protected areas with sandy, silty, or rubbly bottoms and are well known as hard-fighting game fishes.

HAWAIIAN LADYFISH • **awa'aua** • *Elops hawaiensis* •
[HAWAIIAN TARPON; TENPOUNDER]
    Ladyfishes are long, lovely inhabitants of sandy lagoons. Silvery with a golden tinge, especially around the head, they school near the bottom and are easily startled. The mouth is at the tip of the snout and not underslung, as in bonefishes. The Hawaiian Ladyfish often shares habitat with mullets and might be confused with them. They are more slender, however, have one dorsal fin (mullets have two), and do not swim at the surface. Ladyfish occur inside the reef at Hanauma Bay, most predictably in the swimming area at the far right-hand end of the beach, but have been fished out most everywhere else in the Islands. To 2 ft. Endemic to Hawai'i. Photo: Swimming Area.

Hawaiian Ladyfish in Back Door Lagoon (see p.99)

BONEFISH • 'ō'io • *Albula* sp.

Bonefishes have underslung mouths adapted for feeding on bottom-dwelling organisms. Their flesh is full of small bones, hence the common name. Although usually seen inside the reef at Hanauma, often with the Hawaiian Ladyfish, bonefishes also enter deep water. The two Indo-Pacific bonefish species occurring in Hawai'i *(A. glossodonta* and *A. argentea)* appear identical in the field. Neither is common in Hawai'i, possibly due to habitat degradation and overfishing. To about 3 ft. Photo: Swimming Area.

Lizardfishes (Synodontidae)

Like reptilian predators, lizardfishes sit motionless on rocks or sand, blending in almost perfectly with their environment. Propped on their pelvic fins, their heads tilted up for a better view, they often display a grinning mouthful of teeth as they wait for their next victim to swim by. These nasty customers even have teeth on their tongues. Lizardfishes sometimes wriggle into soft bottoms, partially covering themselves. Confident in their camouflage, they will often allow a snorkeler to come close before disappearing explosively in a cloud of sand. Using this powerful acceleration they are able to strike successfully at fishes six or more feet away. Of about 50 species of lizardfishes worldwide, 17 are known from Hawai'i. Looking remarkably similar, they can be difficult to tell apart. In addition to the species below, the larger Slender Lizardfish *(Saurida gracilis)* is sometimes seen inside the reef at Hanauma.

REEF LIZARDFISH • 'ulae • *Synodus variegatus*
This is the lizardfish seen most often by snorkelers and divers in Hawai'i. It prefers rock or coral substrate rather than sand and is splotched with varying shades of red or sometimes greenish or grayish brown. The lips are often banded red and white. At Hanauma Bay it occurs both inside and outside the reef, but only juveniles and subadults are likely to be seen inside. A study conducted (appropriately) at Lizard Island on Australia's Great Barrier Reef showed that on average this fish shifts position every 4 minutes and strikes at prey every 35 minutes. It succeeds only 11% of the time, eating about two fish per day. The species name means "marked with different colors." To about 9 in. Indo-Pacific. Photo: Swimming Area (small juvenile).

Milkfish (Chanidae)

The milkfish family is small, containing only one genus and one species. It falls under the order Gonorhynchiformes, whose members are thought to be related to freshwater minnows and catfishes.

MILKFISH • **awa** • *Chanos chanos*

These are large silvery fishes with a small pointed mouth, deeply forked tail, and a single, almost sharklike dorsal fin. Milkfish grow to 6 ft. in length, although 3 ft. is more typical, and often enter surprisingly shallow areas. They can tolerate brackish or even fresh water but in Hanauma Bay generally frequent the deeper reef habitat, often swimming in midwater well off the bottom. Because of the pointed dorsal fin, snorkelers and divers sometimes mistake them for sharks. The resemblance ends there. Lacking teeth, these fish feed by nibbling algal growths and by filtering microplankton, principally blue-green bacteria, from the water. Occasionally small invertebrates or fish may be taken. Although typically solitary, Milkfish sometimes occur in small groups. Hawaiians once raised them in fishponds, regarding them as highly as the **'ama'ama**, or Striped Mullet. An inexpensive source of protein, Milkfish remain one of the most important cultured food fishes in Southeast Asia. The genus and species names mean "open mouth." The common name refers to the milky white underside. Indo-Pacific and Eastern Pacific. Photo: Palea Point (Zone Three).

Mullets and Threadfins
(Mugilidae and Polynemidae)

Mullets were among the early Hawaiians' most important food fishes. They occur in shallow, often brackish coastal waters and are easily raised in fish ponds. Their long bodies are round or oval in cross section with large scales and two well-separated dorsal fins. They have flattened heads, blunt snouts, and are usually a dull silvery gray. Typically feeding off the bottom, mullets take in sand or mud and filter out the organic material through their gills. Their teeth are minute. About 70 mullet species occur worldwide, with 3 in Hawai'i. Mullets are seldom encountered at snorkeling and diving spots around the Islands, but 2 species are common in Hanauma Bay.

Threadfins, bottom feeders related to mullets, are also highly esteemed table fishes. Their name derives from the threadlike rays of their pectoral fins, which they trail over the sand, apparently to detect food. There are about 29 threadfin species worldwide with 1 in Hawai'i.

STRIPED MULLET • **'ama'ama; 'anae** • *Mugil cephalus*
[GRAY MULLET]
   This is Hawai'i's largest mullet. It is silvery gray with faint stripes along the scale rows. The snout is blunt and the tail fin often edged in black. These fish are common inside the reef at Hanauma Bay but are seldom seen at other snorkeling or diving sites. At home in brackish water, they are easily raised in fish ponds. The ancient Hawaiians had different names for each stage of growth: **pua'ama** (finger length), **kahaha** (hand length), **'ama'ama** (8-12 in.), and **'anae** (full size). Because mullets were highly valued, overly ambitious persons were sometimes told "Don't strive for the **'ama'ama**." (In other words, be satisfied with what you have.) To about 20 in. Found in tropical seas worldwide. Photo: Swimming Area.

SHARPNOSE MULLET • **uouoa** • *Chaenomugil leuciscus*
[FALSE MULLET; ACUTE-JAWED MULLET]

Known locally as False Mullet, or False **'ama'ama,** these fish have a distinctive yellow spot at the base of the pectoral fin and a sharper snout than the larger Striped Mullet (above). They typically swim in small, fast-moving schools, usually grazing directly off the rocky reef rather than the sandy bottom. In Hanauma Bay look for them inside, outside, and over the reef. The young occur in tide pools. The head, if eaten, is said to cause nightmares unless an offering is first made to Pahulu, King of the Ghosts. Older books may place this fish in the genus *Neomyxus*. To about 18 in. Pacific Ocean. Photo: Back Door Lagoon.

PACIFIC THREADFIN • **moi** • *Polydactylus sexfilis*
[SIX-FEELER THREADFIN; KINGFISH]

The silvery **moi** is found over sand bottoms of protected coastlines, usually in small groups, sometimes in large schools. It has a bulbous snout like a cartoon character, an underslung mouth, distinctive swept-back fins, and a deeply forked tail. Unlike mullets, threadfins do not swim at the surface. In old Hawai'i, large schools were said to foretell disaster for **ali'i** (chiefs). Recently this species has been cultured successfully in cages suspended in the ocean offshore. In earlier times it was raised in fishponds. In Hanauma Bay, these fish are sometimes seen inside the reef, usually in the Keyhole Lagoon. The Hawaiian word **moi** also signified a variety of taro and a kind of sweet potato. The species name means "six threads." To about 12 in. Indo-Pacific. Photo: Honolua Bay, Maui.

Needlefishes and Halfbeaks
(Belonidae and Hemiramphidae)

Needlefishes are long, slender, surface-dwelling carnivores with pointed, needlelike beaks filled with sharp teeth. They prey on small schooling fish, which they catch sideways and swallow whole. Some needlefishes dwell in the open ocean; others live close to shore. They are strong swimmers and can skim the surface or leap out of the water. Halfbeaks are similar but with only the lower jaw extended. Many halfbeaks are herbivores, feeding on bits of floating seaweed or other plant material.

Needlefishes and halfbeaks are both related to the flying-fishes or malolo (family Exocoetidae), which are frequently seen from boats as they skim over the surface to escape underwater pursuers. Flying-fishes can glide for distances approaching a quarter mile. Columbus was branded a liar when he first described this feat to the royal court of Spain.

All these fishes have tail fins with the lower lobe longer than the upper, an adaptation helpful in propelling them on the surface. Most are silvery below and bluish on top, a color pattern common among open-ocean (pelagic) fishes that makes them hard to see from both above and below.

Large needlefishes have caused serious injuries. In 1977, a ten-year-old boy fishing with his father from a boat in Hanamalu Bay, Kaua'i, was fatally struck near the eye by a large needlefish that leaped from the water while the boy was pulling in a net. Injuries to snorkelers, however, are virtually unknown.

Hawai'i has at least four needlefish and two halfbeak species. Needlefishes are known in Hawaiian as 'aha ("cord"), and halfbeaks are iheihe or me'eme'e. Juveniles sometimes resemble small twigs floating on the surface. Needlefishes and their relatives belong to the order Beloniformes.

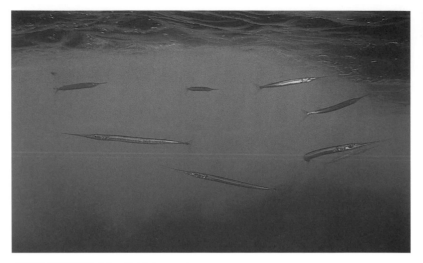

KEELTAIL NEEDLEFISH • 'aha • *Platybelone argalus*
[FLAT-TAIL NEEDLEFISH]

     Schools of these fish are common at many shallow snorkeling areas including Hanauma Bay, especially around the Sandman's Patch area. Sometimes they enter the long cove at the Toilet Bowl where they can be seen from land. Look for them right at the surface. They have a silvery blue stripe along the side. The caudal peduncle (where the tail fin joins the body) is flattened, although this is hard to see. Among them or nearby you may also see the Polynesian Halfbeak *(Hemiramphus depauperatus),* which is shorter and has a long lower jaw tipped with red. To about 15 in. All tropical seas. Photo: Toilet Bowl Cove (Zone Three).

CROCODILE NEEDLEFISH • 'aha • *Tylosurus crocodilus*
[HOUNDFISH]

     Large and heavy-set, with stout toothy beaks and deeply forked tails, these powerful fish grow to more than 3 ft. in length. In Hanauma Bay they often swim just outside the reef, at or near the surface. Occasionally they come inside. They are regular visitors to cleaning stations where Hawaiian Cleaner Wrasses swim up to service them. Capable of leaping free of the water when frightened or attracted by lights at night, these "living javelins" have injured and even killed fishermen in boats with their sharp beaks. To 40 in. All tropical seas. Photo: Kahe Point Beach Park, O'ahu.

Parrotfishes (Scaridae)

With their strong beaks and typically blue-green bodies, parrotfishes are aptly named. Like the wrasses, to which they are closely related, they swim primarily with their pectoral fins and undergo confusing sex and color changes as they mature. Unlike wrasses, parrotfishes are herbivorous. Their teeth are fused into strong, beaklike dental plates, which they use to scrape algae from coral limestone or even to bite off chunks of living coral. This scraping and crunching is easily heard underwater. Small wrasses may hover nearby, hoping to catch bits of food dislodged by the giant as it attacks the substrate. Gouge marks on the coral show where parrotfishes have fed. They actually ingest coral rock, which they grind into fine sand with special bones in the throat. Organic matter is extracted and the sand expelled in a cloud through the anus. (The Hawaiian name for one species means "loose bowels.") It is said that much of the world's coral sand is produced by these fishes.

Parrotfishes are known for their ability to secrete a thick envelope of mucus around themselves at night. The function of this is not clear, and not all parrotfish species do it. Because eels hunt by smell, some biologists believe that this covering protects the sleeping fish from eels during the night. Others suggest that it wards off small crustacean parasites. Parrotfishes are sound sleepers and thus easy to spear at night. Hanauma Bay is an excellent place to see them, for they have been fished out at many other spots.

Parrotfishes are an ichthyologist's nightmare. Anyone who can accurately identify them underwater is a master, for they are fast-moving, shy, and, although extremely variable, often look alike. Color patterns can differ within a species, depending on sex and age, and some species can modify their pattern in seconds. Researchers are still sorting out the different names sometimes erroneously assigned to male, female, and juvenile forms of the same fish. The Bullethead Parrotfish, for example, has had 13 different names in addition to the currently accepted *Chlorurus sordidus*. According to the International Code of Scientific Nomenclature, only the earliest published name is valid. It sometimes takes considerable sleuthing in libraries and museums all over the world to determine who first named a species and when.

In the Hawaiian Islands, parrotfishes are known collectively as **uhu**. In old Hawai'i it was said that the behavior of the **uhu** could tell a fisherman what his wife was doing at home. Hawaiian scholar Mary Kawena Pukui writes, "If the **uhu** capered and frolicked in the water it was a sure sign of too much levity. If two **uhu** seemed to be rubbing noses, it was a sure sign that there was flirting going on at home." A wily person, hard to catch, was called "a slippery **uhu**."

In the descriptions below, references are made to initial- and terminal-phase fishes. In the initial phase most parrotfish species are drab. Mature initial-phase males and females (identical in appearance) sometimes spawn together in large groups, "capering and frolicking." Terminal-phase parrotfishes are always male and usually brightly colored. They hold territories and mate with individual females. These "supermales" are always sex-reversed females.

Seven species of parrotfishes, including three endemics, inhabit Hawaiian reefs. All but two are common in Hanauma Bay.

Star-Eye Parrotfish (terminal male)

Star-Eye Parrotfish (initial phase)

STAR-EYE PARROTFISH • **pānuhunuhu** • *Calotomus carolinus*

Parrotfishes of the genus *Calotomus* have beaks composed of many separate teeth fused together; in other genera the beaks are smooth. Magenta lines radiating from the eyes of terminal males provide easy identification of this species. Their bodies are grayish green to dark green, often with a broad pale patch on the side or irregular pale spots along the back. Initial-phase adults are gray-brown speckled with lighter marks, especially on the back. In Hanauma Bay these parrotfish occur both inside and outside the reef. To 20 in. Indo-Pacific and the Galápagos. Photos: Witch's Brew (Zone Three).

Spectacled Parrotfish (terminal male)

Spectacled Parrotfish (initial phase)

SPECTACLED PARROTFISH • **uhu 'ahu'ula** (initial); **uhu uliuli** (terminal) • *Chlorurus perspicillatus* •

This is the largest of Hawai'i's three endemic parrotfishes. Terminal males are deep blue-green with a conspicuous dark band (the spectacles) across the top of the snout. There is a yellow-green mark at the base of the pectoral fin. Initial-phase fish are grayish brown with a broad white band at the base of the tail (including part of the fin). The fins are red and the fish can rapidly display a series of pale blotches along the back. Body and fins sometimes become uniform gray. These large fish are no longer abundant around the main Hawaiian Islands except in pristine or protected areas such as Hanauma Bay. Most common outside the reef, they also enter the inner areas upon occasion. The Hawaiian name for the initial phase means "feather cape parrotfish." The word **uliuli** applied to terminal males means "any dark color, including the deep blue of the sea." The species name means "spectacled." To 24 in. Endemic. Photos: Boulder Reef (Zone Two).

Bullethead Parrotfish (terminal male)

Bullethead Parrotfish (initial phase)

BULLETHEAD PARROTFISH • **uhu** • *Chlorurus sordidus*

A bullet-shape head profile (symmetrical above and below the beak) marks this species. Terminal males are greenish overall, often with cheeks or sides washed with yellow orange. Initial adults are grayish in front, shading to dark brown, almost black, often with a broad white bar at the base of the tail, which may contain a large dark spot in the center. There is often a double row of three or more white spots on the side and red around the mouth. The species name (describing the initial phase) means "dirty." This is one of the most widespread and common parrotfishes in the Indo-Pacific. At Hanauma Bay large individuals occur mainly outside the reef, although small initial-phase fish are not uncommon inside. To about 15 in. Photos: terminal male—Boulder Reef face (Zone Two); initial phase—Witch's Brew area (Zone Two).

Palenose Parrotfish (terminal male)

Palenose Parrotfish (initial phase)

PALENOSE PARROTFISH • **uhu** • *Scarus psittacus*

Among the most variable of Hawaiian parrotfishes in appearance, terminal males have a green body with lavender tints, sometimes with a large yellow area on the side. When patrolling their territories, they often swim high in the water; the top of their head turns blue-black and a large yellow spot may develop at the base of the tail. Initial adults are plain gray to brownish with a few lighter spots and, sometimes, red pelvic fins. Small compared to terminal males, they typically forage close to the bottom in groups or schools. Despite the common name, the snout of this fish is not much paler than the rest of the body. The species name means "parrot." At Hanauma, the colorful terminal males are seen principally outside the reef, but initial-phase fish are common inside as well as out. To almost 1 ft. Indo-Pacific. Photos: terminal male—Pai'olu'olu Point (Zone Three); initial phase—Witch's Brew area (Zone Two).

Redlip Parrotfish (terminal male)

Redlip Parrotfish (initial phase)

REDLIP PARROTFISH • **uhu palukaluka** (initial); **uhu 'ele'ele** (terminal) • *Scarus rubroviolaceus*

The largest of all Hawaiian parrotfishes, these are common inside the reef at Hanauma, sometimes entering water barely deep enough to cover their backs. When they feed, a Saddle or Christmas Wrasse often follows to nab small creatures dislodged by the grazing giant. Terminal males are light green (darker in front, lighter in back) with a lyre-shape tail fin and a green beak (which often has a "mustache" of dark algae growing on it). The squarish humped snout of large specimens is distinctive. Initial-phase adults are brownish red in front, yellowish gray in back, with numerous short black lines at odd angles on the sides, creating a textured appearance. They may become entirely pale. Their beaks are reddish to white, also with a "mustache." Both initial and terminal phases may display a subtle or distinct bicolor pattern, front half dark, back half light. The common name refers to the initial phase, which alone has red coloration around the mouth. The Hawaiian name for the initial phase means "loose bowels parrotfish" (anyone who has seen a parrotfish eject sand from its anus knows why); the word **'ele'ele**, applied to terminal males, means "black, dark, the black color of Hawaiian eyes." Why this is so is not clear, as their coloration is light. To 28 in. Indo-Pacific and Eastern Pacific. Photos: terminal male—Keyhole Lagoon; initial phase—Back Door Lagoon.

Pufferfishes and Porcupinefishes
(Tetraodontidae and Diodontidae)

When it comes to unusual defensive strategies, few fishes outdo the puffers and porcupinefishes. Although belonging to different families, their techniques are similar—puffers have bristly skins, while porcupinefishes are completely covered with sharp spines. When alarmed, both distend themselves with water into prickly balloons to discourage attack and to make themselves difficult, or impossible, to swallow. If removed from the sea they inflate with air, to the accompaniment of little croaking noises.

Inflating into a spiny or bristly ball is not their only defense; these fishes are also poisonous. The little tobies, or sharpnose puffers, of the genus *Canthigaster*, with limited powers of inflation, secrete a substance from their skin making them immediately unpalatable to predators. But more importantly, most of these fishes accumulate in their internal organs and in other parts of their bodies a poison called tetrodotoxin, one of the most interesting and powerful neurotoxins known. Tetrodotoxin may or may not be dangerous to other fishes, but it is deadly to humans. It causes tingling, numbness, and eventual paralysis. Sometimes a curious state of "living death" ensues, wherein the victim retains consciousness while unable to move, or even breathe. True death may occur within 24 hours. In spite of this, or perhaps because of it, pufferfishes are delicacies in Japan, where specially licensed fugu chefs prepare them safely for the table. The flesh is said to be firm, white, and sweet; the small residue of poison produces a highly prized warmth or "glow."

Like the closely related boxfishes, puffers and porcupinefishes have chunky bodies that lack both scales and pelvic fins. They are comparatively weak swimmers but nevertheless roam freely over the reef, primarily by waggling dorsal and anal fins set far back on the body. Except for the small colorful tobies, they do not appear to have territories. These fishes range greatly in size, from the tobies that rarely exceed 4 in. to the large porcupinefishes that attain almost 3 ft. Equipped with sharp beaks and powerful jaws, they are capable of eating almost anything that doesn't swim away. They can also deliver a painful bite. Some puffers feed by squirting a jet of water at the sandy bottom to uncover buried organisms.

Both puffers and porcupinefishes belong to the order Tetraodontiformes, which also includes boxfishes and triggerfishes. The Hawaiian names for these fishes are the subject of debate. The popular word **makimaki**, a corruption of **make** ("death"), was probably not used in ancient Hawai'i. The fishes called **'o'opu hue** ("stomach like a gourd"), or kēkē ("potbelly") were probably puffers. The majority of Hawai'i's puffers, mostly small tobies, have no known Hawaiian names. All told, 12 puffers and 3 porcupinefishes inhabit our waters. Snorkelers in Hanauma Bay are most likely to see the 4 below.

SPOTTED PUFFER • **'o'opu hue** • *Arothron meleagris*
[GUINEAFOWL PUFFER]
  This chunky puffer is about a foot long and brown or black covered with numerous small white spots. Two other color phases occur rarely: all yellow with a few dark spots, and partly yellow, partly brown, with dark or white spots. It is found near coral, upon which it feeds. In Hanauma Bay, look for it outside the reef. The bristly skin feels like velcro, especially when the fish is inflated. The species name means "guineafowl," an African bird covered with white spots. To about 13 in. Indo-Pacific. Photo: Back Door Lagoon.

AMBON TOBY • *Canthigaster amboinensis*
  These chunky dark tobies display iridescent blue-green lines and spots and are quite pretty when seen in bright light. Occurring singly or in pairs, they inhabit shallow, bouldery areas both inside and outside the reef and also among corals. They are fast swimmers for tobies and can be difficult to approach. The species is named for the Indonesian island of Ambon. To about 5 in. Indo-Pacific. Photo: Mākua, O'ahu.

HAWAIIAN WHITESPOTTED TOBY • *Canthigaster jactator* •
Covered with white spots and often displaying a slight green fluorescence, these are by far the most common Hawaiian tobies. They usually occur in pairs and in Hanauma Bay are common both inside and outside the reef. Occasional individuals have irregular black marks on the snout and body. These cute but mischievous puffers will stealthily approach other fishes and nip their fins, leaving perfect semicircular "cookie-bites" along the edges. Although they seem shy by nature, their species name means "boaster" or "braggart." To 3 1/2 in. Endemic. As with most Hawaiian endemics, these fish have close relatives similar in appearance elsewhere in the Pacific. Photo: Back Door Lagoon.

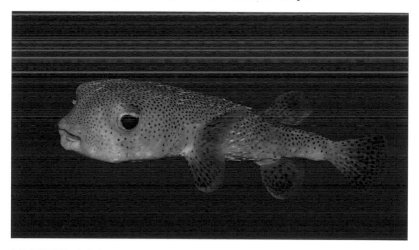

PORCUPINEFISH • kōkala • *Diodon hystrix*
The large head and eyes of this fish make its flabby, tapering body seem emaciated in comparison. Spines lie flat along the entire body, which is covered with small black dots. Like many others in its family, it is nocturnal. By day it typically rests alone under a ledge or hovers quietly in some protected area, often in small aggregations well off the bottom. The largest of the porcupinefishes, in Hanauma Bay it occurs most commonly outside the reef. The Hawaiian name means "spiny." The species name means "porcupine." To 28 in. All tropical seas. The similar but slightly smaller Spiny Porcupinefish (*D. holocanthus*) also occurs both inside and outside the reef at Hanauma. Photo: Mahi wreck, Leeward O'ahu.

SPOTTED BURRFISH • **kōkala; ʻoʻopu hue** • *Chilomycterus reticulatus*

This rare fish has similar proportions to *Diodon hystrix* (above) and attains almost the same size. The coloration, too, is similar—gray on the back with scattered small dark spots lightening to white underneath, and many dark spots on the fins. Unlike *D. hystrix,* it may have diffuse dark bars below the eye and on the sides. The biggest difference, however, is in the spines. Short and permanently erect, they resemble thorns of a rose. Like others in its family, this fish is most active at night. By day it generally hovers quietly in caves and under ledges. It occurs in warm seas throughout the world, most commonly in subtropical and warm temperate regions. In Hawaiʻi it is seen most predictably in the northwestern chain; in the main islands it is rare. At Hanauma Bay, however, it is not uncommon, generally outside but sometimes inside the reef. It attains about 22 in. Photo: near Sandman's Patch.

Rays

Cousins to the sharks, but totally unlike them in appearance, rays have flattened bodies, great winglike pectoral fins, and often a long thin tail. Like sharks, the skeleton is cartilaginous, they have gill slits instead of gill covers, and their mouth is usually on the underside. Most rays swim by rippling their large pectoral fins, but some use their pectoral fins like wings, "flying" gracefully high in the water and sometimes leaping into the air.

Best known are the stingrays (family Dasyatidae), which bear one or more venomous spines near the base of their tail and often bury themselves in sand. At Hanauma stingrays never venture close to shore, nor do the huge manta rays (family Mobulidae), but Spotted Eagle Rays (family Myliobatidae) are not uncommon. Of about twenty-four species of eagle rays, one occurs in Hawai'i. The two general names for rays in Hawaiian are **lupe**, which also means "kite," and **hīhīmanu**, "magnificent."

SPOTTED EAGLE RAY • **hailepo; hīhīmanu** • *Aetobatus narinari*
Eagle rays have a distinct head, triangular "wings," and an amazingly long, slender tail that often greatly exceeds the length of the body. Although they feed by foraging in the sand for shellfish and other organisms, they spend much of their time "flying" well above the bottom, sometimes in groups. One of the most beautiful of all underwater sights is a formation of eagle rays flying together in synchrony. On a calm day, advanced snorkelers at Hanauma Bay might glimpse one or two of these magnificent animals patrolling the reef in deeper waters beyond the Witch's Brew. They grow to over 6 ft. wide and occur in all tropical seas. In olden days this species was forbidden to women as food. Photo: Kahe Point, O'ahu.

Scorpionfishes and Gurnards
(Scorpaenidae and Dactylopteridae)

Scorpionfishes are slow-moving or sedentary carnivores, many with venomous spines that can deliver a painful sting. Some, like the dreaded stonefishes, are masters of camouflage almost impossible to detect; others, such as the lionfishes, may have conspicuous colors and enlarged fins that enhance visibility. Most scorpionfishes fall into the hard-to-detect category. They rely on dull, mottled coloration and rough-looking, spiny, warty or tasseled skins to escape notice. Many harbor algae and other growths in their skins, the better to blend with their environment and possibly even to attract prey. Some scorpionfishes have the ability to periodically shed these growths along with the cuticle, or outermost layer of skin.

Scorpionfishes sting. If threatened, many bring into play venomous spines on the dorsal, anal, and pelvic fins. In some scorpionfishes the spines are connected to a sac of venom at their base. In others the poison glands lie beneath a sheath of skin covering the spines. In either case, punctures can be extremely painful. Stepping on or touching a highly camouflaged scorpionfish is always a possibility while snorkeling, although they do not seem to be at all common inside the reef at Hanauma Bay. If stung, the best treatment is immediate immersion of the affected area in hot, but not scalding, water for 30 to 90 minutes (heat destroys the protein venom). Bleeding should be encouraged. If pain is severe, seek medical care.

The family Scorpaenidae (one of about 20 families in the order Scorpaeniformes) includes about 350 species worldwide. Twenty-five species occur in Hawai'i; one is pictured here. The general name for scorpionfishes in Hawaiian is **nohu**. The peculiar Flying Gurnard from the related family Dactylopteridae is also included in this section.

DEVIL SCORPIONFISH · nohu ʻomakaha · *Scorpaenopsis diabolus*

These are the scorpionfish encountered most often on Hawaiʻi's reefs. Usually they sit in the open, their skin texture and color exactly matching the surroundings, whether coral rubble, smooth rounded stones, or algae-covered reef. (Living coral, however, is not in their repertoire and they generally avoid sitting on it.) These masters of deception harbor algae and perhaps other growths in their skin, the outermost layer of which they shed from time to time. They have a distinctly humped back and, surprisingly, sport bright yellows and oranges on the underside of their pectoral fins. When disturbed, a Devil Scorpionfish will move a few feet, flashing the normally hidden colors. Predators stung while attacking one will remember the "flash" and not repeat the mistake. At Hanauma Bay these fish usually occur outside the reef, although occasionally one is seen inside. They never fail to fascinate snorkelers alert enough to spot them. The specimen pictured was sitting on sand and easy to see, unusual for the species. The species name means "devil." To 12 in. Photo: Sandman's Patch.

FLYING GURNARD · loloaʻu; pinao ·
Dactyloptena orientalis
[HELMET GURNARD]

Flying Gurnards do not fly; they crawl along sandy bottoms using the specially modified fingerlike spines of their pelvic fins. When alarmed they spread their "wings" (an enormous pair of pectoral fins) thus blending with the bottom and greatly increasing their apparent size. Ordinarily the "wings" are kept folded along the side of the armored, boxlike body. Flying Gurnards are occasionally encountered in sandy channels in the reef environment. Inside the reef at Hanauma Bay they occur in areas of mixed sand and rubble. Unlike scorpionfishes, they are not venomous. Photo: Swimming Area

Sharks

Are there sharks in Hanauma Bay? Yes, a few. They are typically shy of humans and you'd be lucky to see one. (Your best chance is in the early morning.) Whitetip Reef Sharks and Blacktip Reef Sharks are most likely to be seen, but Scalloped Hammerheads and Gray Reef Sharks have occasionally been reported. There are no records of sharks attacking humans in the bay.

Sharks, along with the rays, skates, chimaeras, and ratfishes, belong to an evolutionary branch of fishes having skeletons of cartilage instead of bone. They perfected their form about 60 million years ago and have changed little since. Instead of the gill covers typical of modern bony fishes they have 5-7 gill slits on each side. Their tough skins lack scales; shark skin is so rough to the touch that it has sometimes been used as sandpaper. This roughness is caused by embedded dermal denticles much like small teeth. Sharks' teeth, in fact, are special dermal denticles enlarged and modified.

With the exception of a few large plankton-eaters, such as whale sharks, all sharks are carnivores. While smaller species may subsist on molluscs, crustaceans, or other less exciting fare, in the main these are swift, sleek, streamlined creatures superbly suited to a predatory life. Few animals, and certainly no other fishes, have so captured the human imagination or excited such admiration and dread.

Sharks are known as manō in Hawaiian. In olden days, and even into the present, individual sharks were believed to physically embody the spirits of certain family ancestors. These family gods (aumākua) were given regular offerings of food (their haunts were well known) and in return, the sharks were said to protect their worshipers. The story is often told of the Pearl Harbor drydock, that, despite warnings from native Hawaiians, was constructed in 1913 over the known home of a sacred shark. When almost complete, the entire structure collapsed. A kahuna was brought in to bless the site, and a new dry-dock (this time a floating one) was completed without further trouble. When it was finished the skeleton of a 14-foot shark was found underneath.

In the main Hawaiian Islands, sharks generally avoid humans. Except for the two inoffensive species described below, snorkelers and divers rarely see them. Because of massive and sometimes senseless human predation, coupled with their own slow rate of reproduction, shark populations worldwide are rapidly dwindling. The word "shark," from the same root as "shirk," originally meant scoundrel or villain.

BLACKTIP REEF SHARK • **manō pā'ele** • *Carcharhinus melanopterus*

These sharks have distinct black tips or black margins on all fins; those on the first dorsal fin and lower lobe of the tail fin are the most conspicuous. Skittish and inoffensive, Blacktips are not considered dangerous. Once common in Hawai'i, they are seldom seen today. These are shallow-water sharks that frequent reef flats and lagoons where they feed on fishes, octopuses and crustaceans. Juveniles sometimes cruise the shallows in water only inches deep. In Hanauma Bay, your best chance of seeing a Blacktip is in the early morning outside the reef. It will probably vanish as soon as it sees you. The species name means "black fin." The Hawaiian name means "dark" or "black." To almost 6 ft. Photo: Maui Ocean Center.

WHITETIP REEF SHARK • **mano lālā kea** • *Triaenodon obesus*

This is the only shark seen with any regularity on Hawaiian reefs. The body is grayish brown and the tips of the first dorsal and upper tail fins are white. Usually encountered resting on the bottom in caves or under ledges, these sharks hunt at night and are adept at pursuing fishes and crustaceans into the recesses of the coral. The same sharks probably frequent the same caves over a period of time. Although they appear lethargic, they are not harmless and should not be trifled with. Whitetips sometimes enter Hanauma Bay and on occasion are seen just outside the reef or even in Sandman's Patch or the Back Door Lagoon, usually in the early morning. When they see a human they typically depart. If you find a shark, treat it with respect and consider yourself fortunate! Although the species name means "fat," this is a comparatively slender shark. To about 6 ft. Indo-Pacific and Eastern Pacific. Photo: "Ewa Pinnacles," O'ahu. This is a young Whitetip only a few feet long.

Snappers and Emperors (Lutjanidae and Lethrinidae)

Perchlike carnivores of considerable economic importance, snappers are common on shallow tropical reefs throughout the world. Most species native to Hawai'i, however, inhabit depths greater than 200 ft. These include the Pink Snapper and the Red Snapper ('**opakapaka** and **onaga**), some of the Islands' best-loved food fishes. The two native shallow-water snappers—solitary predators sometimes known as jobfishes—are not abundant enough to be of major commercial value. To stimulate the fishing industry, three species of reef-dwelling snappers from the South Pacific and Mexico were introduced to the State of Hawai'i in the 1950s and early 1960s. The Blacktail and Bluestripe Snappers, described below, have become common; the third, the Paddletail Snapper *(Lutjanus gibbus),* is rare.

Little thought was given in earlier years to the ecological effects of these introductions. We now suspect that valuable shallow-water food fishes such as the Whitesaddle Goatfish, or **kūmū** (p.87), are being displaced by the introduced Bluestripe Snapper, or **ta'ape**. This voracious fish also ranges into deeper waters; when fishermen set their lines for valuable '**ōpakapaka**, schools of ta'ape often steal the bait. Unfortunately, Bluestripe Snappers have a low market price and their introduction has been a commercial failure.

About 100 snapper species are known worldwide, varying in length from about 10 in. to 3 ft. The larger snappers are usually solitary, while the smaller species typically school by day, dispersing at night to feed on small fish and crustaceans. Hawai'i has 14 snappers (including the 3 introduced species). The 2 below are common in Hanauma Bay.

The emperors are closely related fishes that, until recently, were classified in the snapper family. Hawai'i's one emperor is included in this section.

BLUESTRIPE SNAPPER · **ta'ape** · *Lutjanus kasmira*　　　　　　　　　　　→

Yellow with four narrow, bright blue longitudinal stripes, these showy snappers are a common sight around reefs and wrecks. They rest during the day in large schools that frequent same spots year after year. Although introduced to Hawai'i from the Marquesas in 1958 for commercial reasons, they have been a flop in island markets and are often regarded by fishermen as a pest rather than an asset. Investigations suggest that these aggressive feeders consume mostly small crabs, outcompeting valuable **kūmū** and other native goatfishes that rely on the same prey. They have now spread up the Hawaiian chain as far as Midway and Kure Atolls. In Hanauma Bay a small school is almost always present in Sandman's Patch, inside the reef. The Tahitian name, **ta'ape**, has come into common use in Hawai'i. To 15 in., but usually smaller. Indo-Pacific. Photo: Sandman's Patch.

BLACKTAIL SNAPPER • **to'au** • *Lutjanus fulvus*
[FLAMETAIL SNAPPER]

These handsome snappers are grayish yellow with a red dorsal fin and a black tail fin that becomes red at the edges. The pectoral and anal fins are yellow. Adults usually remain close to the bottom and are solitary. Juveniles are abundant among the mangroves of Kāne'ohe Bay, O'ahu. The species was introduced to Hawai'i from Mo'orea, French Polynesia, in 1956 but is not as common around reefs as the Bluestripe Snapper (below). Apparently these fish are wanderers. Shortly after their original release off O'ahu in Kāne'ohe Bay, Blacktail Snappers were captured both in Waimea Bay and off Honolulu, each a good 27 miles away! In Hanauma Bay they occur both inside and outside the reef. The species name means "tawny." **To'au** is the Tahitian name. To 13 in. Indo-Pacific. Photo: Back Door Lagoon.

Bluestripe Snappers (see previous page).

BIGEYE EMPEROR • mū • *Monotaxis grandoculis*
    These lovely fish have large, dark eyes and blunt snouts. Adults are entirely silvery but can darken to a pattern of three broad dark bars on the upper half of the body. Smaller individuals usually show the barred coloration, with some yellow about the head and lips. Bigeye Emperors feed at night and hover by day in midwater off the face of the reef, rippling their fins gently to maintain a position facing into the current. Juveniles, usually seen closer to the bottom, have a pointed snout and a more highly contrasting barred pattern. **Mū** have teeth that resemble human molars. In old Hawai'i, a man sent to find victims for live burial beside the body of a chief was also called **mū**. Children, of course, were told that if they were bad the **mū** would get them. In Hanauma Bay these occur only outside the reef. To almost 2 ft. Indo-Pacific. Photo: "Ammo Reef" (off Wai'anae Boat Harbor), O'ahu.

Soldierfishes and Squirrelfishes (Holocentridae)

Fishes of the family Holocentridae are small to medium-size nocturnal predators, usually red, with big scales, a deeply forked tail fin, and large, dark eyes. All rest by day, generally under ledges and in caves, and hunt freely over the reef at night. Their red color is typical of many nocturnal and deep-water fishes, actually making them more difficult to see. Because red wavelengths are rapidly absorbed by water, red becomes equivalent to black at night or in deep water.

There are two groups in this family: the squirrelfishes (subfamily Holocentrinae) and the soldierfishes (subfamily Myripristinae). Both are common in Hawai'i, and at least five species occur inside the reef at Hanauma Bay. They hide during the day, however, and only the two most likely to be seen are pictured here. The name "soldierfish" may come from the epaulette-like shoulder bars and the red coloration, reminiscent of British redcoats. In Hawai'i, soldierfishes are often called by their Japanese name, *menpachi*. The Hawaiian name is 'ū'ū.

Despite their perchlike appearance, squirrelfishes and soldierfishes do not belong to the order Perciformes as do most of the fishes in this book. Their more primitive anatomy places them in the order Beryciformes, of which they are the only members common on coral reefs. They range in length from about 3-18 in. The family name Holocentridae means "all spiny" or "all prickly."

Mixed group of Hawaiian Squirrelfish and Bigscale Soldierfish

BRICK SOLDIERFISH • 'ū'ū •
Myripristis amaena

This is the only Hawaiian soldierfish whose soft dorsal, anal, and tail fins are plain red without white edges. The body is brick red. Preferring depths less than 25 ft., it is the species most likely to be seen by snorkelers in Hanauma Bay. Look for it in hollow spaces in and under the reef, both inside and outside. It leaves the shelter of the reef at night to feed on plankton. The Pearly Soldierfish (*M. kuntee*) and the Bigscale Soldierfish (*M. berndti*), both similar in appearance to the present species, also occur inside the reef. To about 10 in. Restricted to the Pacific islands. Photo: Sandman's Patch. (Two Yellowfin Goatfish are also visible).

SPOTFIN SQUIRRELFISH • 'ala'ihi • *Neoniphon sammara*

Most squirrelfishes are red; this one is silvery with brownish red stripes following the rows of scales. A dark red spot is visible on the dorsal fin when it is raised. Shy and retiring, this squirrelfish does not congregate in large groups as often as its relatives. At night a red stripe appears on the upper side. The smaller, endemic, red Hawaiian Squirrelfish (*Sargocentron xantherythrum*) is also glimpsed from time to time in holes and under deep ledges inside the reef. To 10 in. Indo-Pacific. Photo: Sandman's Patch.

Surgeonfishes and Moorish Idols
(Acanthuridae and Zanclidae)

Surgeonfishes, or tangs, are probably the most numerous and conspicuous Hawaiian reef fishes. Each surgeonfish bears two knifelike spines or scalpels at the base of its tail fin—one on each side. Ordinarily these scalpels lie flat in a groove, but a swipe of the tail will flip one out, ready for action against enemy or intruder. In unicornfishes (which belong to the surgeonfish subfamily Nasinae) the scalpels are replaced by extremely sharp fixed bony projections. In either case, these fishes are capable of causing serious injury to predators or rivals. The common name "surgeonfish" was inspired by the deep, painful cuts they occasionally inflict on careless humans, typically while being removed from a net or spear. But don't blame the fish—its scalpels, or the areas around them, are often brightly colored as a warning. In some species the scalpels and fin spines are mildly venomous, causing wounds that are slow to heal. Well-behaved divers and snorkelers, however, have little to fear from surgeonfishes.

Surgeonfishes are typically oval, with thin (compressed) bodies and scales so small as to seem nonexistent. They propel themselves with winglike beats of their pectoral fins, as do wrasses and parrotfishes. Although a few species feed on plankton, most are algae eaters with mouths adapted for either scraping the surface of rocks and dead coral or nibbling leafy seaweeds.

Because algae grow best in bright light, most surgeonfishes are shallow-water creatures. Some, such as the mid-size Achilles Tang and Whitespotted Surgeonfish, inhabit the turbulent surge zone. Smaller species, such as the Convict Tang and Brown Surgeonfish, prefer calmer waters, often browsing the reef in large mixed schools. Moving together in a group affords protection from predators and, more importantly, enables them to overcome the territorial defenses of other algae-eating fishes. One of these is the Pacific Gregory, an aggressive and common little damselfish that vigorously defends its own patch of algae against individual intruders. It can only dart about in helpless frustration when several hundred peacefully grazing surgeonfishes sweep through its territory. Some larger species, such as Yellowfin and Ringtail Surgeonfish, feed on the almost microscopic film of algae growing on compacted sandy bottoms.

Unlike other surgeonfishes, many unicornfishes grow a long horn on the forehead. Some are plankton-eaters that school well above the bottom, often in deeper water than other surgeonfishes. Although there appears to be no Hawaiian name for surgeonfishes in general, the unicornfishes are all known as **kala**, which also means "thorn." In old Hawai'i a person who could well defend himself was praised as "a **kala** fish with a sharp tail." The family name, Acanthuridae, originates in the Greek word *akanthos* ("thorn").

Of the 23 species of surgeonfishes and unicornfishes that occur in Hawaiian waters, 16 are described here. Included also is the closely related Moorish Idol, the only member of the family Zanclidae. Moorish Idols lack a scalpel and resemble butterflyfishes in appearance and behavior. A careful observer, however, will note that, like surgeonfishes (and unlike butterfly-fishes), they swim largely with their pectoral fins. Their family name is from the Greek *zanclon* ("sickle").

ACHILLES TANG • **paku'iku'i** • *Acanthurus achilles*

An orange, teardrop-shape patch over the scalpel identifies this surgeonfish; the body is black. Common along rocky shores with moderate wave action, these active fish seem to spend much of their time driving away intruders. A short charge and a sudden turn to expose a scalpel does the job nicely. When agitated, their bodies and flared fins take on a reddish glow. Sometimes a white patch develops under the pectoral fins. The Greek warrior Achilles symbolizes youthful grace, beauty and valor. To make him invulnerable, Achilles' mother held her baby by the heels and dipped him in the River Styx. The fingerprint-like orange marks inspired the species name. The Hawaiian name refers to a method of scaring fish into nets by slapping and pounding the water. In Hanauma Bay these fish are most abundant outside the reef but occur inside as well. To 10 in. Restricted to the islands of the Pacific. Photo: Back Door Lagoon.

Goldrim Surgeonfish

GOLDRIM SURGEONFISH • *Acanthurus nigricans*
[WHITECHEEK SURGEONFISH]

Slightly smaller than the Achilles Tang, but otherwise similar in habits and appearance, these have yellow around the scalpel and along the base of the dorsal and anal fins. The white tail fin contains a narrow yellow bar. When agitated they flare their fins, outlining their body with gold. The fins, in turn, are edged with electric blue. Although uncommon in Hawai'i, snorkelers at Hanauma can see these fish inside the reef in the vicinity of the Back Door Channel. This species and the more common Achilles Tang sometimes reproduce together; at least one hybrid with orange in its tail fin inhabits the Back Door Channel area too. The species name means "blackish." To 8 in. Islands of the tropical Pacific and Eastern Pacific. Photos: Pai'olu'olu Point (Zone Three); hybrid—Back Door Lagoon.

Goldrim Surgeonfish/Achilles Tang hybrid

WHITESPOTTED SURGEONFISH • 'api • *Acanthurus guttatus*
These fish have an almost circular brown body with white bars in front and many white spots in back. The pectoral fins are intense yellow. A long sloping snout terminates in a thick upper lip. Inhabiting turbulent, rocky shores, these fish are adept at riding the foamy surge into the shallows to nibble for a few seconds at algae before being swept back into deeper water. They usually occur in small groups but sometimes browse the reef in large schools. At Hanauma Bay they are most common along the outside of the reef and in surge areas on top of the reef. The species name means "spotted." To 11 in. Indo-Pacific. Photo: Sandman's Patch.

WHITEBAR SURGEONFISH • **māikoiko** • *Acanthurus leucopareius*
Easy to identify, this species has a prominent white bar behind the eye; the body is grayish brown. When feeding it often schools, sometimes with the Convict Tang. It is most common close to shore in turbulent areas, at Hanauma especially around the sides and near the mouth of the bay in Zone Three. It occurs inside the reef too, but not as abundantly. The species name means "white cheek." To 10 in. Restricted to the subtropical Pacific islands. Photo: Sandman's Patch.

BROWN SURGEONFISH · mā'i'i'i · *Acanthurus nigrofuscus*
[LAVENDER TANG]

These shallow-water surgeonfish are grayish brown but with a definite lavender tinge, especially on the fins. Dull orange spots dot the head. There are small dark spots above and below the base of the tail. Common and drab, few snorkelers pay them much attention, but they are interesting nonetheless. In some locations, such as inside the reef at Hanauma Bay, they are territorial, defending small areas primarily against other herbivores, especially the Convict Tang. In other places they behave quite differently, browsing the reef in large schools, often *with* Convict Tangs. At some sites they spawn daily from February to October in huge aggregations. Finally, the largest bacteria known to science live in their gut, apparently aiding digestion. In Hanauma Bay these fish occur both inside and outside the reef. The species name means "dark," the Hawaiian name, "tiny." To 8 in. Indo Pacific. Photo: Kahe Point Beach Park, O'ahu.

BLUELINE SURGEONFISH · maiko ·
Acanthurus nigroris

Common reef fish, these are dark brownish gray with fine, somewhat wavy blue lines running lengthwise along the body and two small dark spots above and below the base of the tail. Like some other surgeonfishes they can change color to almost black, often with a white ring around the tail. The blue lines, however, always remain faintly visible. These fish are slightly larger than the Brown Surgeonfish (above), with which they might be confused. At Hanauma Bay they occur both inside and outside the reef. The species name means "blackness." To 10 in. Pacific islands. Photo: Back Door Lagoon.

CONVICT TANG • manini • *Acanthurus triostegus*
Possibly the most abundant fish in the bay, Convict Tangs are light greenish or yellowish white with six black bars (the convict's stripes). They often browse the reef in large dense schools thereby overwhelming the defenses of aggressive, territorial herbivores such as Achilles Tangs, Brown Surgeonfish, and Pacific Gregories. At Hanauma Bay feeding schools often form both inside and outside the reef but these fish also browse singly or in small groups. Juveniles occur in tide pools and inlets, even where the water is brackish. Only in Hawai'i does this species have the narrow, oblique bar under the pectoral fin. For this reason the Hawaiian population is given the subspecies name *sandvicensis*. Although **manini** were a favored food fish in old Hawai'i, the popular name has come to mean undersized or stingy. To 10 in. Indo-Pacific and Eastern Pacific. Photo: Reef Face (Zone Two).

ORANGEBAND SURGEONFISH
na'ena'e • *Acanthurus olivaceus*
Adults of this surgeonfish always have a short orange band rimmed in blue on their shoulder. They can rapidly change body color from light olive to cleanly divided light and dark to completely dark. Often browsing in groups, they occasionally join other surgeon-fishes in large, mixed schools. They feed both over sand and hard sub-strate, unusual for their family. Smaller juveniles, bright yellow without an orange band, might be confused with the Yellow Tang. At Hanauma Bay these fish occur both inside and outside the reef but are most common outside. The species name means "olive color." To 12 in. Pacific Ocean. Photo: Palea Point (Zone Three).

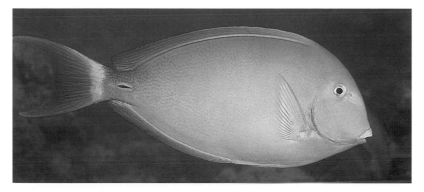

YELLOWFIN SURGEONFISH · **pualu** · *Acanthurus xanthopterus*

One of two large surgeonfishes that share the Hawaiian name **pualu**, this species is purplish gray with yellow and blue banded dorsal and anal fins and a deep blue, lyre-shape tail. It sometimes turns almost completely dark with a white ring around the tail. No matter what its color, the outer third of the pectoral fins is always yellow, giving both its common and scientific names. (These yellow pectorals help to distinguish it from the Ringtail Surgeonfish, also called **pualu**, whose pectorals are dark.) The tail spine of the Yellowfin Surgeonfish is black, distinguishing it from another similar fish, the Eyestripe Surgeonfish or **palani**. When fish feeding was allowed at Hanauma, Yellowfin Surgeonfish were abundant inside the reef. Dozens would swarm around anyone offering food, outcompeting most other contenders because of their size. The natural habitat of these fish, however, lies in deeper water where they feed on thin films of algae growing on compacted sand. They have become less abundant inside the reef and eventually may leave entirely. To 22 in. Indo-Pacific and Eastern Pacific. Photo: Back Door Lagoon.

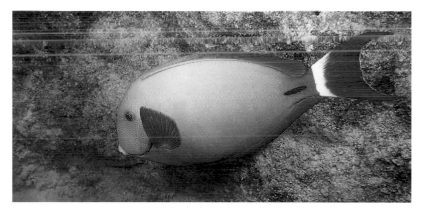

RINGTAIL SURGEONFISH · **pualu** · *Acanthurus blochii*

This surgeonfish may be dark overall or bluish gray with dark blue dorsal and anal fins; it usually has a white ring around the tail. Neither the body color nor the white ring is a good identifier, however, because the similar Yellowfin Surgeonfish—which shares the Hawaiian name **pualu**—can adopt this color pattern. To positively identify the Ringtail, look at the pectoral fins, which are always dusky, never yellow. The natural habitat of this fish lies in deeper water outside the reef, where it feeds on the thin film of algae growing on compacted sand. Fish feeding over the years has drawn it into the shallower areas near shore. Although feeding has stopped, it remains common inside the reef. Someday, though, it may move out for good. The name honors German ichthyologist M.E. Bloch (1723-1799) who described many species in this book. To 17 in. Indo-Pacific. Photo: Sandman's Patch.

EYESTRIPE SURGEONFISH • **palani** • *Acanthurus dussumieri*

A white scalpel immediately separates the **palani** from the similar Yellowfin and Ringtail Surgeonfishes (above). The fish can alter its color from light blue to almost black, often with a white ring around the tail. The dorsal fin is a beautiful ochre color. Large specimens have an unusually large, rounded snout. This fish often rests under ledges. Its natural habitat is in deeper water outside the reef where it feeds on the thin film of algae growing on compacted sand. Fish feeding over the years attracted it into the shallower areas near shore, but it is not as common as the two fishes above. The **palani** has a strong odor when cooked; a Hawaiian riddle based on this name means "odor reaching to heaven." Because of the association with bad smell, the word also came to mean "detested person" or "outcast." To 18 in. Indo-Pacific. Photo: Telephone Cable Channel.

GOLDRING SURGEONFISH • **kole** • *Ctenochaetus strigosus* •
[GOLDRING BRISTLETOOTH]

The **kole** has a bright gold ring around the eye. The dark to light gray body is marked with many fine horizontal lines, and the mouth is surrounded by blue. In old Hawai'i these fish were placed under the posts of a new home to ensure good luck. At Hanauma Bay it is one of the ten most common fishes both inside and outside the reef. The species name means "thin" or "meager." The Hawaiian name means "raw" (which is how it was eaten). To 7 in. The Goldring Surgeonfish was for many years considered to have an Indo-Pacific distribution, although with several regional variations. A recent study by Dr. John E. Randall of the Bishop Museum has shown that it is endemic to Hawai'i and that three similiar species inhabit other areas of the Pacific. Another common name for surgeonfishes of the genus *Ctenochaetus* (the first "c" is silent) is "Bristletooth." Photo: Reef Face (Zone Two).

YELLOW TANG • lauʻīpala • *Zebrasoma flavescens*

Except for a white tail spine, these beauties are entirely bright yellow. A school of them flowing over the reef is a sight unique to Hawaiʻi; although ranging as far as Japan and Guam, the species is abundant only here. Juveniles, thin and delicate as wafers, have greatly elevated dorsal and anal fins. Unlike adults, they do not school and are especially common in stands of Finger Coral. Snorkelers in Hanauma Bay will have no trouble finding Yellow Tangs outside the reef; they occasionally occur inside as well, especially in the channels. Beyond the Witch's Brew, in Zone Three, they often form large feeding schools, typically with Convict Tangs and other surgeonfishes. The species name means "yellow," the Hawaiian name, "yellowed leaf." To almost 8 in. Hawaiʻi, Marshall Islands, Mariana Islands, Southern Japan. Photo: Midway Atoll.

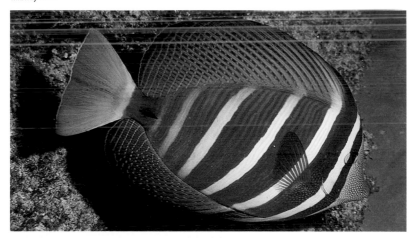

SAILFIN TANG • māneoneo • *Zebrasoma veliferum*

Named for their remarkable, sail-like dorsal and anal fins, these lovely large surgeonfish are banded brown, yellow, and white. The tail fin is yellow and the spine is surrounded by dark blue. If alarmed, these fish extend their fins, greatly enlarging their apparent size. Adults often swim in pairs or trios, occasionally in schools. They are common both inside and outside the reef at Hanauma. Juveniles have high, permanently extended fins but are almost never seen. The scientific name means "carrying a sail." When eaten raw, some fishes cause an unpleasant sensation in the throat. This may be one; the Hawaiian name means "itchy" or "irritating." To 15 in. Indo-Pacific. Photo: Back Door Lagoon.

PALETAIL UNICORNFISH • **kala lōlō** • *Naso brevirostris*
[SPOTTED UNICORNFISH]

These unicornfish have a horn and a white tail fin containing a darkish spot. Large adults have small spots or lines on their sides. These fish swim well off the bottom and feed on plankton. Large specimens with long horns usually occur over deep water near the entrance to the bay, while subadults with shorter horns are common just outside the reef. They frequently swim with Sleek Unicornfish (below). Juveniles lack a horn and, unlike adults, eat leafy seaweeds. As the horn lengthens it eventually prevents the mouth from reaching the substrate, forcing them to adopt a planktonic diet! The inaccurate species name means "short-horned." Perhaps the original specimen was not fully grown. The Hawaiian word **lōlō** means "lazy" or "crazy." To 24 in. Indo-Pacific. Photo: Molokini Islet, Maui.

SLEEK UNICORNFISH • **kala holo; ʻōpelu kala** • *Naso hexacanthus*

These hornless unicornfish are uniform in color and can change almost instantly from a metallic blue-gray to entirely dark. The tail fin has a bluish sheen. Plankton-eaters, they aggregate in midwater, often with the Paletail Unicornfish (above). Groups of three or four often descend to be serviced by Hawaiian Cleaner Wrasses. (When its turn comes to be cleaned, a Sleek Unicornfish usually pales to light blue, perhaps making parasites stand out.) In Hanauma Bay these fish are seen only outside the reef. Sometimes they form large dense schools, probably for spawning. The Hawaiian word **holo** means "swift." To 30 in. Indo-Pacific. Photo: Palea Point (Zone Three).

ORANGESPINE UNICORNFISH · umaumalei · *Naso lituratus*

Orange lips, a graceful curve of yellow from eye to mouth (somewhat like a **lei**), and bright orange tail spines identify this attractive hornless unicornfish. Common in shallow water, it feeds on fleshy algae. Large males have tail streamers. When chasing another fish the dull yellow mark on the forehead becomes intensely yellow, looking almost like a headlight. View these fish from above to fully appreciate the wicked, bright orange, forward-curving tail spines. Snorkelers at Hanauma Bay can see these fish both inside and outside the reef. They often occur in pairs. The species name means "blotted out" or "blurred." The lovely Hawaiian name combines **umauma** ("chest") and **lei** ("garland"). To 18 in. Indo-Pacific. Photo: Back Door Lagoon.

BLUESPINE UNICORNFISH · kala · *Naso unicornis*

These large unicornfish sport a long horn and sharp, fluorescent blue tail spines. Males have tail streamers. Small specimens lack the horn. While resting over sand they are light brownish gray, but when browsing on algae they often darken except for a light shoulder patch. Their horns are recessed, unlike those of the Spotted Unicornfish, enabling them to crop algae from the substrate. This is the only horned unicornfish seen inside the reef at Hanauma Bay. When resting over the sand it is wary and difficult to approach, but when browsing the reef it may allow you to tag along. Despite the lack of bright colors, this is an attractive large fish when seen at close range. The Hawaiian name means "thorn." In old Hawai'i its tough skin was used for making drums. To 27 in. Indo-Pacific. Photo: Sandman's Patch.

MOORISH IDOL • **kihikihi** • *Zanclus cornutus*

Moorish Idols, with their perfect blend of form and color, are the classic coral reef fish. Living symbols of the exotic undersea world, they have light gold bodies marked with jet-black bands, long orange and white striped snouts, and graceful trailing filaments. Moorish Idols often swim in pairs, occasionally in small schools, and to view them underwater is always a delight. At Hanauma Bay they occur most commonly outside the reef, but you will see them inside as well. Although unrelated, they are remarkably similar to Pennant Butterflyfish (p.65), which are rarely seen by snorkelers at Hanauma Bay. The Hawaiian name ("curves," "corners," "angular," "zigzag") was applied to a number of fishes, including hammerhead sharks. To about 8 in. Indo-Pacific and Eastern Pacific. Photo: Swimming Area.

Triggerfishes (Balistidae)

Triggerfishes are named for the unusual arrangement of their two dorsal spines. The first spine, thick and strong, can be erected and locked into place internally with the second spine, which is shorter. At the slightest danger, most triggerfishes dive into a hole or crevice and erect these spines, making themselves very difficult to remove. It is said that if the second spine (the "trigger") is depressed, the locking mechanism will release, and the surprised triggerfish can be pulled from its refuge. This procedure is not recommended, however, as surprised triggerfishes can deliver a nasty bite. In Hawaiian, triggerfishes are called **humuhumu** ("to stitch pieces together"), perhaps referring to the geometric pattern on one common species.

Triggerfishes have tough skins and small but strong jaws and mouths with which they feed on crustaceans, echinoderms, coral, or almost anything edible. Because their eyes are placed far back on the body, some seem to be at least half head. Many triggerfishes are plankton-eaters. All swim by rippling their soft dorsal and anal fins. This enables them to move backward as well as forward, an advantage while maneuvering in and out of small spaces. They deposit their eggs in nests on the bottom, where they are guarded, usually by the female. Some species routinely charge and even bite humans who approach their nests. In Hawai'i this is highly unusual, although nesting Reef Triggerfish inside the reef at Hanauma Bay have on rare occasions bitten snorkelers who approached too close. If a triggerfish swims at you aggressively, back off. You are too near its nest.

Triggerfishes belong to the order Tetraodontiformes, which includes other curious fishes such as the filefishes, pufferfishes, and boxfishes. Of perhaps 20 Indo-Pacific species, 10 are known from Hawai'i and 5 described here.

BLACK TRIGGERFISH • **humuhumu ʻeleʻele** • *Melichthys niger*
[BLACK DURGON]
These fish are dark, almost black, with two conspicuous light blue lines along the bases of the soft dorsal and anal fins. When agitated they display a radiating pattern of iridescent blue lines between the eyes. Black Triggerfish often aggregate above the bottom, feeding on plankton and drifting algae. At Hanauma Bay they occur only outside the reef, where they are abundant in certain areas, especially along the right side of the Bay beyond the Witch's Brew. In old Hawaiʻi these fish were sometimes burned as fuel when wood was scarce. Both the species and the Hawaiian names mean "black." To about 1 ft. Occurring in tropical seas worldwide, this is one of the few reef fishes found in both the tropical Atlantic and Pacific oceans. Triggerfishes of the genus *Melichthys* are also known as durgons. Photo: beyond Witch's Brew (Zone Three).

PINKTAIL TRIGGERFISH · humuhumu hiʻu kole · *Melichthys vidua*
[PINKTAIL DURGON]

These fish are dark brown with clear to whitish anal and soft dorsal fins and a white and pink tail. Although they do not school, their habits are similar to those of the Black Triggerfish (above). Snorkelers in Hanauma Bay will see them only outside the reef. The species name means "widow," the Hawaiian name, "raw tail" or "red tail." To about 13 in. Indo-Pacific. Photo: Finger Coral reef (Zone Three).

LAGOON TRIGGERFISH · humuhumu-nukunuku-ā-puaʻa · *Rhinecanthus aculeatus*

This species has a beautiful blue hat, yellow lips bordered with blue, and a yellow bridle. There is much black on the upper body, and diagonal white bands on the lower rear side. When viewed from above, a bull's-eye-like mark is conspicuous on the fish's back. Rows of rough, file-like spines at the base of the tail face outward as protection when the fish retreats into a hole (true of all *Rhinecanthus* species). Preferring a sandier, weedier habitat than the similar Reef Triggerfish (next page), it is less common but somewhat easier to approach. At Hanauma Bay this triggerfish is seen only inside the reef. It has the same Hawaiian name as the following species. To 1 ft. Indo-Pacific. Photo: Swimming Area.

REEF TRIGGERFISH • **humuhumu-nukunuku-ā-puaʻa** • *Rhinecanthus rectangulus*
[PICASSO TRIGGERFISH]

 Colored lines, geometrically arranged, give this curiously patterned fish one of its common names, Picasso Triggerfish. The position of its eyes, high and about one third of the way down the tan body, enables it to attack long-spined sea urchins. Although common on shallow reef flats, it is one of the most difficult fishes to approach or photograph. The descriptive words **nukunuku- ā-puaʻa** mean "nose like a pig" and the fish grunts like a pig when pulled from the water. The famous song "My Little Grass Shack" features this fish. According to legend, the pig demigod **Kama-puaʻa** once escaped the wrath of the volcano goddess **Pele** by turning into a triggerfish. Legend also relates that in the guise of a triggerfish he once saved some children from a shark. Schoolchildren and others across the state returned the favor in 1984 by electing the **humuhumu** Hawaiʻi's State Fish. Fish experts argued in favor of other species, but children's **hula** groups dancing to the tune of the famous song captured the hearts of the voters. Out of some 60,000 votes cast—some from as far away as Maine, Massachusetts, and Arizona—the triggerfish won with 16,577, followed by the **manini** (8,742), the **lauwiliwili nukunuku ʻoiʻoi** (8,543), and the **hīnālea lauwili** (6,206). The story, however, does not end there: Displeased with the election, certain fish experts persuaded the Legislature to limit the **humu**'s term to five years! Its term has now elapsed, but so far no one has suggested a successor to this popular fish. At Hanauma Bay it occurs both inside and outside the reef. Despite a normally shy disposition, a nesting Reef Triggerfish will on rare occasions charge and even bite snorkelers who get too close. If a triggerfish swims right at you, back off. To 10 in. Indo-Pacific. Photo: Cable Channel (Zone Two).

LEI TRIGGERFISH · humuhumu lei · *Sufflamen bursa*
[WHITELINE TRIGGERFISH]

Two curved bands, like strands of a lei running up from the base of the pectoral fin, give this fish its name. The bands may be brown, gray, or yellow. The body is grayish brown and white. A thin white line runs diagonally from mouth to anal fin. These triggerfish usually occur singly, but it is not uncommon to see a pair closely circling or chasing each other (often high off the bottom) in some sort of territorial or sexual encounter, with one or both fish making clearly audible grunting sounds. At Hanauma Bay look for these outside the reef, although occasionally they venture inside. To 8 1/2 in. Indo-Pacific. Photo: Palea Point (Zone Three).

Trumpetfishes and Cornetfishes
(Aulostomidae and Fistulariidae)

These remarkably long predators are among the most-asked-about fishes in Hanauma Bay. They can be seen hovering over the reef almost any time, but in the early morning or late afternoon they become especially active, carefully stalking small fishes and literally sucking them into their tubelike mouths with an often-audible "whomp." Their mouths are capable of enormous expansion, permitting them to swallow fishes as large or larger in diameter as themselves.

The stiff, sticklike trumpetfishes are solitary, but the sinuous cornetfishes occasionally group together. Trumpetfishes have vertically narrow (compressed) bodies; cornetfishes are horizontally flattened with a long filament extending from the tail fin. Both belong to the order Syngnathiformes (tubemouthed fishes), which includes the pipefishes and seahorses. One species of each is known from Hawai'i.

Both of these fishes owe their common names to a fancied resemblance to musical instruments and are sometimes called flutemouths. Their family names derive from *aulos* ("flute") and *fistula* ("pipe"). In Hawaiian they are known as **nūnū** or **nuhu**.

CORNETFISH • **nūnū** • *Fistularia commersonii*
Cornetfish have a long, whiplike filament extending from the center of the tail. Their flattened bodies are greenish, with light blue lines and dots on the back. To blend with their surroundings they can rapidly assume a pattern of dark bars. Unlike Trumpetfish, Cornetfish flex from side to side as they swim. They may hunt in small groups and often swim high in the water or over sand. At Hanauma they are more common than Trumpetfish inside the reef. The species name honors the famous French naturalist Philibert Commerson (1727-1773). To 4 1/2 ft. (including the tail filament). Indo-Pacific. Photo: Back Door Lagoon.

Yellow coloration

Normal coloration

TRUMPETFISH • **nūnū** • *Aulostomus chinensis*

Inflexible and sticklike, these fish are usually gray or brown, sometimes with pale vertical bars or longitudinal stripes; in Hawai'i a bright yellow color phase is common. They have a barbel on the chin that may serve as a lure and swim by fluttering dorsal and anal fins set far back on the body. Trumpetfish are probably the most common fish predators on Hawaiian reefs. Sneaky hunters, they ambush or stalk their prey, maneuvering slowly and carefully within striking range, often from a vertical position. Although conspicuous from the side, Trumpetfish are almost impossible to see from the perspective of their prey—head on. They sometimes hunt by swimming closely alongside another fish, such as a puffer or parrotfish, or by accompanying schools of surgeonfishes. When swarms of Milletseed Butterflyfish attack a patch of Hawaiian Sergeant eggs, a yellow trumpetfish will often turn up, taking advantage of its color and the general confusion to nab a small fish or two. Another tactic these fish use is to align themselves with some long, thin object such as a rope or anchor line, thereby hoping to go unnoticed. In this photo, however, a young inexperienced Trumpetfish is aligning itself with a larger one. It probably won't catch much that way. Photo: Sandman's Patch.

Wrasses (Labridae)

Old Woman Wrasse

No account of coral reef fishes could be complete without the wrasses. At most snorkeling sites these often colorful characters are almost unavoidable. Slender and fast moving, they seem to fly through the water with winglike beats of their pectoral fins. Although a diverse group, most wrasses are elongated, cigar-shape fishes with one continuous dorsal fin. The Hawaiian Islands, with 43 species, are an excellent location for observing them.

Characteristic of the family are bright, gaudy color patterns, which vary dramatically with age and sex. Because of this, wrasses have been one of the most difficult families to classify. For many years males and females of some were thought to represent completely separate species. The same was true for adults and juveniles. To add to the confusion, dominant males ("terminal males" or "supermales") of some species are more vividly colored than ordinary males. For this reason, rather than separating wrasses by sex it is often more helpful to divide them into "initial" and "terminal" growth phases.

The initial phase can consist solely of females or of both sexes, depending on species. Most adult wrasses are initial-phase fish. They look alike and are reproductively mature. If both sexes are present, they are capable of spawning together in a group. Comparatively few initial-phase wrasses enter the terminal phase.

Terminal-phase wrasses are always male. Though less numerous, they are more noticeable due to their brighter colors. Terminal-phase males are dominant; they typically hold a territory and spawn individually with the females within it.

These social arrangements may be complex, but they are flexible; many wrasse species are able to change from female to male to suit the needs of the group. If the dominant male is removed, for example, the largest or most aggressive initial-phase female reverses sex and assumes his role. In fact, all terminal-phase males begin life as females. Wrasses "born" male never become dominant and are doomed to a life of mediocrity.

Wrasses have thick lips and their sharp teeth often project slightly forward and are easily seen. They are carnivorous, typically preying upon small invertebrates. One Hawaiian wrasse feeds primarily on fish, several others on planktonic animals. Possibly the most unusual with respect to feeding habits are the small, colorful cleaner wrasses, which pick parasites from the skin and gills of other fishes. Cleaners inhabit a specific territory, such as a ledge or coral head, and attract attention by swimming up and down with a distinctive dancing motion. Any fish pausing at the cleaning station will get serviced by them. They even clean inside the mouths of large fishes with impunity.

Most wrasses are small to mid-size, the biggest Hawaiian species growing to about 20 in. During the day they depend on speed and agility to escape predators; at night they seek refuge in holes and cracks, or bury themselves in the sand. A few species spend the night in tide pools.

The general Hawaiian name hīnālea is applied to most (but not all) wrasses; many of the smaller varieties have no known Hawaiian names. In old Hawai'i a pungent condiment was made using partially decomposed wrasses, crushed kukui nuts, and chili pepper; a person with bad breath was sometimes referred to unkindly as "a dish of hīnālea sauce."

The family name comes from the Greek name *labros*, also meaning "greedy." The word "wrasse" derives from either the Celtic *urach* or the Cornish *gwragh* (take your pick). With over 600 species, the wrasses form a very large family, second only to the gobies. Hawai'i has forty-three species, thirteen of them endemic. The nine seen most often by snorkelers in Hanauma Bay are described below.

Pearl Wrasse (male)

Pearl Wrasse (female)

PEARL WRASSE • 'ōpule • *Anampses cuvier* •

Initial-phase Pearl Wrasses (females) are dark with reddish undersides and are decorated with lines of white dots like strings of pearls. Terminal males are dull blue-green with brighter blue markings on the head and tail, sometimes with a light vertical bar on the side. Seen most often in rocky areas close to shore, these fish also enter deeper water. They feed by striking the bottom forcefully with the mouth to dislodge small prey, creating a sound similar to that of a parrotfish feeding. The species name honors French biologist Baron Georges Cuvier (1769-1832), who originally described a number of fishes in this book. The Hawaiian name means "variegated in color." To 14 in. Endemic to Hawai'i. Photos: Swimming Area.

YELLOWTAIL CORIS • **hinalea 'akilolo** • *Coris gaimard*
[Rainbow Wrasse]

Like living rainbows, initial adults have a green-blue body speckled with brilliant blue spots, a bright yellow tail, and orange-red dorsal and anal fins edged with electric blue. Terminal males are darker, often with a lighter vertical bar down the center of the body. Juveniles are bright orange-red with a series of white saddles along the top of head and back. At Hanauma Bay these wrasses are likely to be seen only outside the reef. The Hawaiian name means "brain-biting" (the fish was used in the treatment of head diseases). The species name honors Paul Gaimard (1796-1858), naturalist and officer on the French ship *Uranie,* which visited Hawai'i in 1819. Gaimard helped collect and describe the first scientific specimens of many fishes in this book. At Hanauma these fish generally live outside the reef. Males to about 15 in., females smaller. Indo-Pacific. Photo: female—Portlock Point, O'ahu.

ELEGANT CORIS • *Coris venusta* •

Somewhat dull in color, these wrasses are apt to be overlooked. When they spread their fins in bright light, however, they live up to their name. Males and females are similar, with males more colorful. Males have a yellow crescent-shape mark above the pectoral fin. Juveniles have a wide brownish stripe on the head and front half of the body. At Hanauma Bay you can find these fish both inside and outside the reef. They are named after Venus, goddess of beauty. To about 7 in. Endemic to Hawai'i. Photo: male—Back Door Lagoon.

Bird Wrasse (male)

Bird Wrasse (female)

BIRD WRASSE • **hīnālea ʻiʻiwi** (male); **hīnālea ʻakilolo** (female) • *Gomphosus varius*
 Bird Wrasses are easily identified by their long curved snout, which they use to nab small invertebrates from crevices or from between branches of coral. Terminal males are dark green with a bright green patch by the pectoral fin; initial-phase adults are white in front, darkening to black. Active fish, they are always on the go. In Hanauma Bay can be seen both inside and outside the reef. The species name means "different." The Hawaiian name for the terminal phase refers to the **ʻiʻiwi**, or Scarlet Hawaiian Honeycreeper, an endemic bird with a long curved bill. The initial-phase name means "brain biting," possibly because these fishes were used in the treatment of brain diseases. To 12 in. Pacific Ocean (with a similar species, *G. coeruleus,* in the Indian Ocean). Photos: male— Witch's Brew area; female—Sandman's Patch.

HAWAIIAN CLEANER WRASSE • *Labroides phthirophagus* •

These small, beautiful wrasses make their living by picking parasites, and perhaps dead tissue, from the bodies of larger fishes. Adults are yellow, blue and magenta with a black stripe from head to tail; juveniles are black with an intense blue line along the back. They set up permanent "cleaning stations" on the reef, typically near a prominent coral head or under a ledge, where they service their customers. During busy periods, other fishes may actually line up to wait their turn. At Hanauma Bay, Hawaiian Cleaner Wrasses are common inside and outside the reef. Inside, cleaning stations are typically under ledges in the deeper areas of the lagoons. The impossible-to-pronounce species name means "louse eater." To 4 in. Endemic. Photo: Back Door Lagoon.

A Hawaiian Cleaner Wrasse services an Achilles Tang at Palea Point (Zone Three). Another tang waits its turn. While being cleaned, fish often change color, perhaps to make parasites stand out.

Belted Wrasse (terminal male)

Belted Wrasse (initial phase)

BELTED WRASSE • ʻōmaka • *Stethojulis balteata* •

Possibly the prettiest of Hawaiian wrasses, terminal males of this species are mostly green with several vivid blue lines on head and body and a broad orange stripe from pectoral fin to tail. The dorsal fin is bright orange. Drab by comparison, and less often noticed, initial-phase adults (both sexes) are grayish with a bright yellow spot at the base of the pectoral fin. These wrasses are fast-moving and always on the go. At Hanauma Bay look for them both inside and outside the reef. The species name means "girdled." To almost 6 in. Endemic to Hawaiʻi. Photos: terminal male—Palea Point (Zone Three); initial phase—Kahe Point Beach Park, Oʻahu.

Old Woman Wrasse (terminal male)

Old Woman Wrasse (initial phase)

OLD WOMAN WRASSE · **hīnālea luahine** · *Thalassoma ballieui* •
[BLACKTAIL WRASSE]

These large, rather plain wrasses have little fear of humans. Initial-phase adults (both sexes) are grayish with a thin, vertical reddish line on each scale. Pastel yellows and blues mark the pectoral fins and the anal fin is pastel pink. Terminal males are similar with a darker head, dark pectorals, dull blue under the chin, and a black tail. Juveniles are bright green. The name honors Théo Ballieu, a French diplomat in Honolulu at the time of King Kalākaua. The Hawaiian name means "old woman." To about 15 in. Endemic. Photos: terminal male—Reef Face (Zone Two); initial phase—Back Door Lagoon.

Christmas Wrasse (terminal male)

Christmas Wrasse (initial phase)

CHRISTMAS WRASSE • 'āwela • *Thalassoma trilobatum*

These fast-moving wrasses inhabit shallow reefs, often in the surge zone, where they feed mostly on crabs and molluscs. Terminal males have bright, ladderlike blue-green markings on a reddish body and bright blue pectoral and tail fins. No photo can do justice to their kaleidoscopic colors seen in bright sunlight. The brown and green initial-phase adults (both sexes) are smaller and drab by comparison. At night these fish sometimes sleep in pools just above the water line where they can be discovered by flashlight. Juveniles live in tide pools. At Hanauma Bay, this species is common both inside and outside the reef. To about 11 in. Indo-Pacific. Photos: terminal male—Sandman's Patch; initial phase—Back Door Lagoon.

SADDLE WRASSE · **hīnālea lauwili** · *Thalassoma duperrey* •

These are the most abundant wrasses in Hawai'i, and one of the most common fishes inside the reef at Hanauma Bay. Initial adults (both sexes) are blue green with a dull orange band behind the head. Terminal males are similar with a crescent-shape (lunate) tail fin and a whitish area behind the orange band, which they can "turn on and off." Juveniles are lighter, lack the orange band, and have a dark stripe running from snout to the tail through the eye. Juveniles sometimes clean other fish, somewhat like the Hawaiian Cleaner Wrasse (p.151). The species name honors physicist Louis Isodore Duperrey (1786-1865), 2nd lieutenant of the French ship *Uranie* which visited Hawai'i in 1819. The Hawaiian name means "turning" or "twisting." To 10 in. Endemic. Photo: terminal male—Back Door Lagoon.

ROCKMOVER WRASSE · *Novaculichthys taeniourus*
[DRAGON WRASSE]

Juveniles, popularly called Dragon Wrasses, are among the most unusual fishes on the reef. The filamentous extensions on their fins and an almost continuous swaying and twisting motion help them resemble drifting seaweed. Adults lose the filaments, becoming dark with white marks on each scale (appearing grayish at a distance) with a white bar through the tail. (A subadult is pictured here—about halfway between the juvenile and adult form.) These fish are usually seen nosing about sandy or rubbly bottoms, large ones sometimes actually moving or overturning rocks in search of prey. Although uncommon, they occur both inside and outside the reef. The species name means "ribbonlike." To 12 in. Indo-Pacific and Eastern Pacific. Photo: subadult—Swimming Area.

SEA TURTLES

A Green Turtle hovers over a Finger Coral reef in Zone Three while Goldring Surgeonfish clean algae off its shell. Photo: D.R. & T.L. Schrichte.

The first "walking fishes" are believed to have crawled up on land about 350 million years ago. Over time these animals developed lungs and legs; some evolved into the scaleless amphibians (frogs, toads, and salamanders) while others retained scales and became reptiles. The amphibians remained partially aquatic, but the reptiles mastered terrestrial life and dominated the earth for millions of years. Perhaps competition on land became too fierce, for about 150 million years ago some reptiles re-entered the ocean. Among their descendants are today's crocodiles, sea snakes, and sea turtles. Of these, only sea turtles occur regularly in Hawaiian waters; sea snakes are extremely rare.

All turtles are characterized by a tough shell that protects the entire body—top, bottom, and sides. The shell covering the back is called the carapace, and the shell on the underside is the plastron. Freshwater turtles can retract their heads into their shells, but sea turtles cannot. They have flippers instead of legs, and use their front pair to pull themselves through the water breast-stroke fashion. Powerful swimmers, they spend almost their entire lives at sea. Some species undertake migrations of 1,000 miles or more. Like other reptiles, sea turtles breathe air and during normal activity must surface every few minutes; when resting they can remain underwater for over two hours.

A sea turtle's only essential tie to land is reproductive (although Hawaiian Green Turtles sometimes bask on shore). Females of all species return to their natal beach every few years to nest. Laboriously, in the dark of the night, they pull themselves above the high tide line and excavate a shallow body pit by flinging away sand with their flippers, taking several hours to do so. They then scoop out a deep, round egg chamber in the moist sand using their back flippers and drop in 100-200 eggs, one by one. Finally they cover the egg chamber, fill in all traces of their night's work, and drag themselves back down to the sea by dawn.

The young hatch in about two months, emerge from the sand at night, make their way down the beach, swim out through the waves, and begin their lives in the open sea. Although this ancient reproductive cycle worked well for millions of years, it leaves sea turtles extremely vulnerable today. All seven of the world's species are in peril. Loss of nesting habitat is the primary cause, as an increasing human population encroaches on or destroys their traditional nesting beaches. Even where they nest unhindered, people dig up the eggs (prized as an aphrodisiac by some cultures), and animals, wild and domestic, prey on the young hatchlings. Under good conditions probably only one hatchling in about a thousand lives to maturity.

Adult sea turtles face new dangers of their own. They often entangle themselves in fishing nets and drown, or die after eating plastic bags and other floating debris, which they probably mistake for jellyfish. Humans in many parts of the world hunt turtles either for meat or for their shells. In recent years large numbers of Green Turtles, the most common species, have died from a tumor-causing viral disease known as fibropapillomatosis, which seems to be most prevalent in areas of high human population. Turtles with tumors on their heads and necks are sometimes seen in Hanauma Bay. They will almost certainly die in a year or two unless a treatment can be devised.

In the United States, sea turtles are protected by the 1973 Endangered Species Act. It is illegal to take or harass them. Never pursue a sea turtle or attempt to make contact with it. In particular, "riding" a turtle can quickly exhaust it and prevent it from surfacing to breathe. Imagine someone trying to "ride" you as you come up for air!

In most parts of the world, just seeing a sea turtle is a rare experience. Not so in Hawai'i, where Green Turtles are quite common. Snorkelers in Hanauma Bay see them regularly, even inside the reef. These animals will often ignore humans who swim gently or just float in their vicinity. Divers and advanced snorkelers sometimes encounter a Hawksbill Turtle or two in deeper water near the entrance to the bay. The giant oceangoing Leatherback Turtle, which can weigh up to 1,500 pounds, occurs in off-shore Hawaiian waters but has not been reported in Hanauma. In the Hawaiian language, all turtles are called **honu**.

GREEN TURTLE · **honu** · *Chelonia mydas*

Green Turtles are the most widespread and numerous of Hawai'i's marine turtles. Adults feed mostly on algae, generally grazing along shore in the early morning and late afternoon. It is common to see them at Hanauma Bay, both inside and outside the reef. When not feeding they often rest, seemingly asleep. Active Green Turtles must surface to breathe every few minutes; when resting they can remain underwater for two hours or more. Turtles tend to rest in "traditional" areas, either under ledges and in caves or directly on the reef. One such area lies on a Finger Coral reef at the Witch's Brew side of the bay in about 30 ft. of water. Here up to about half a dozen turtles can be found at a time lying in individual depressions they have made in the coral over the years. Traditional cleaning areas also exist where turtles come to have surgeonfishes (usually Goldring Surgeonfish, but sometimes Brown Surgeonfish, Achilles Tangs, Sailfin Tangs, or Yellow Tangs) eat the algae off their shells. Sometimes Saddle Wrasses will pick parasitic barnacles off their skin. Hawaiian Green Turtles are unusual in that they sometimes bask on land during the day. Few other sea turtles do this. Basking behavior is most common in the Northwestern Hawaiian Islands and on parts of the Big Island, such as the black sand beach at Punalu'u. It has not been seen at Hanauma. Basking turtles conserve energy and avoid predation by sharks (generally Tiger Sharks).

When male Green Turtles reach maturity at perhaps age 25, they grow a conspicuous long heavy tail. Immature males and females have quite short tails. In Hawai'i, adult Green Turtles of both sexes migrate periodically to their nesting beaches, which are almost always at French Frigate Shoals, an atoll in the Northwestern Hawaiian Islands. After mating offshore, females crawl up on the beach at night to dig a pit and deposit their eggs. They do not nest every year, but when reproductively active they may nest up to five times in a season. After hatching in about two months, juvenile Green Turtles remain at sea for about a year feeding on jellyfish and other surface-dwelling animals.

Green Turtles in Hawai'i have been protected under Hawai'i State Law since 1974; in 1978 they were listed as threatened under the federal Endangered Species Act. It is illegal to take or harass them. If you see a turtle, swim gently or just float and it will likely ignore you and allow you to get quite close. If you see a resting turtle, do not disturb it. Never pursue or attempt to touch a sea turtle. Although the dark brown shells of these animals may be greenish from a coat of algae, Green Turtles get their name from the greenish color of their fat, evident to cooks in years past who butchered them for turtle soup, considered a delicacy. These animals reach a length of about 4 ft. but the average adult in Hawaiian waters is probably about 3 ft. Maximum weight is about 400 lbs. The species occurs worldwide in warm seas. The name *mydas* means "wet." Some authors give the subspecies name *agassizi* to Hawaiian Green Turtles, but this is not generally accepted. Photos: Boulder Reef (Zone Two).

See photos on opposite page ⟶

Green Turtle

Green Turtle

HAWKSBILL TURTLE • 'ea; honu 'ea • *Eretmochelys imbricata*

Hawksbill Turtles are uncommon in Hawai'i, but at least two individuals have frequented the Hanauma Bay vicinity for years. As their name implies, Hawksbills have narrow, pointed bills that are easily distinguished from the blunter bills of Green Turtles, and the scale pattern on their heads and flippers often seems more conspicuous. Except on very young or very old individuals, the edges of the carapace are slightly serrated due to the large overlapping scutes (scales); adult Green Turtle shells, by contrast, are smooth along the edge. In Hawai'i, Hawksbills nest principally on the main islands, making them more vulnerable than Greens. Only a handful of their nesting beaches—mostly on the Big Island and on Moloka'i—remain undisturbed. The nesting season extends from late May through November. Hawksbill Turtles are omnivores, feeding mainly on sponges and other marine invertebrates that grow on hard substrate, using their pointed bills to probe into crevices. They are listed as endangered under the Endangered Species Act and are also protected under Hawai'i State Law. It is illegal to take or harass them. Unfortunately, their shells are attractive when polished and in some parts of the world a considerable market exists for "tortoise shell" products such as combs and souvenirs. It is illegal to bring such items into the United States. The species name *imbricata* means "overlapping" in reference to the scutes (scales) on the carapace. The Hawaiian word 'ea ("reddish brown") refers to the color of the shell. Adult Hawksbills attain a length of about 3 ft. and weigh up to 270 lbs. Males have longer, thicker tails than females. Hawksbill Turtles range worldwide in tropical seas. Photos: Lāna'i Lookout, O'ahu.

WHAT IS AN INVERTEBRATE?

Any animal without a backbone is an **invertebrate.** Over 90 percent of animals fall in this category, including the insects, crabs, shrimps, snails, slugs, clams, octopuses, worms, sea stars, sea urchins, sponges, and a host of lesser-known creatures. They exist in enormous variety, especially in the sea. Animals with backbones are called **vertebrates.** Although more familiar to us, vertebrates form only a small minority of Earth's living creatures. They include mammals, birds, fishes, reptiles, and amphibians. Being vertebrates ourselves, we humans tend to lump the invertebrates together as a group. In truth, however, they form no natural group; the various types of invertebrates are as different from each other as we are from them. The category "invertebrate," therefore, is mostly one of convenience.

The invertebrate animals most likely to be encountered by snorkelers in Hanauma Bay include stony corals, zoanthids (or colonial anemones), sea urchins, sea cucumbers, spaghetti worms, and octopuses. Crabs, shrimps and lobsters, and many sea snails, although present, hide during the day and are seldom seen in the open. Broad groups of invertebrates (and other organisms) are placed in large groupings called **phyla** (singular **phylum**). A phylum is then subdivided into **classes, orders, families, genera** (singular **genus**), and species. The same binomial nomenclature used for fishes is used for invertebrates and all other living organisms. This section is organized alphabetically by phylum.

Cnidarians • Phylum Cnidaria (Coelenterata)

Cnidarians (pronounced without the "c") are simple, multicelled animals consisting basically of a stomach and a mouth. Some books call them coelenterates. Sea anemones, jellyfishes, hydroids and corals belong to this group. All have radially symmetric, saclike or bell-shape bodies open at one end. Stinging tentacles usually surround the opening to collect food and provide protection. In many cnidarians a hard external skeleton cradles the soft body and positions the animal advantageously with respect to currents or light. Cnidarians may be solitary or colonial. Those most likely to be seen in Hanauma Bay are stony corals, zoanthids, and occasionally box jellyfishes.

Stony Corals

Stony corals are cnidarians that secrete limestone skeletons. Individual animals are called polyps. Polyps are generally small (only 1/25 to 1 in. in diameter) and are typically interconnected to form colonies. Their individual cuplike skeletons, called calyces (singular, calyx), also join to form solid structures of many shapes and sizes, including branching fingers, bushes, lobes, and mounds. Large colonies, often called "heads" or "bommies," may be hundreds of years old and attain heights of about 25 ft. The accumulated skeletons of coral polyps, cemented together by limestone-secreting coralline algae, form coral limestone—the underlying basis of living coral reefs. The great atolls and barrier reefs of the Pacific Ocean consist of coral limestone deposits up to 5,000 ft. thick. These reefs are the largest structures on Earth made by living organisms.

Living coral colonies are completely covered by a thin double layer of tissue that connects the polyps and allows them to share nutrients. This tissue layer also secretes skeletal material between the calyces, prevents fouling organisms from overgrowing the skeleton, and hosts the symbiotic algae that give colonies their color—usually brown, yellow, or olive. Excess sugars manufactured by symbiotic algae are the main food of most reef-building corals, although they also capture small planktonic animals with their tentacles. The reliance of reef-building corals upon symbiotic algae requires that they live in warm, clear, relatively shallow water where there is plenty of sunlight.

Hawai'i has about 60 species of shallow-water corals in 17 genera, low numbers compared with the many hundreds of species, in about 80 genera, occurring around Indonesia and the Philippines. Uplifted fossil reefs on O'ahu and other Hawaiian islands indicate that more species of corals existed here in the geological past. (Pieces of coral embedded in the tuff walls of Hanauma Bay might be examples too.) Hawaiian waters today are too cool for the vigorous growth of many tropical species, and wave action along most exposed coasts is too strong to allow corals to accumulate into reefs. In Hawai'i, true coral reefs form only in protected bays such as Hanauma or along usually calm leeward coasts. Actually, much of the "coral limestone" in the Islands is the work of limestone-secreting plants called coralline algae, which flourish in shallow, turbulent water where corals do not thrive.

General Hawaiian names for coral include 'āko'ako'a, ko'a, and puna. In ancient times stony coral skeletons were used as abrasives for smoothing canoes and rubbing off pig bristles; Mushroom Coral was a favorite.

Bleached white coral skeletons (**puna kea**) were also placed on fishing shrines and used to mark paths across dark lava flows.

Snorkelers in Hanauma Bay will see the most living coral outside the reef, but those who remain inside and look carefully will find a surprising variety of species, especially in the Back Door Lagoon and Sandman's Patch. All eleven species illustrated here were photographed *inside* the reef at Hanauma. Coral colonies inside the reef generally live on vertical or near-vertical surfaces. Exceptions are some heads of Evermann's Coral in the Back Door Lagoon and some small Lace Coral colonies in depressions along the top of the reef. Be careful of these living corals. Avoid grabbing them or knocking them with your fins. One person might not do measurable damage, but the cumulative impact of thousands of visitors could be harmful. Only about 1 percent of the fringing reef at Hanauma is covered with living coral. For the most part this is its natural condition, not a result of human impact. Some large, completely dead mounds of Lobe or Evermann's Coral in Sandman's Patch and elsewhere, however, were clearly alive in the not too distant past, as evidenced by snapping shrimp channels on their surfaces (see p.176). Most likely these dead coral heads were casualties of sediment caused by the blasting in 1956 and later.

LACE CORAL • *Pocillopora damicornis*

This shallow-water coral forms small bushy heads up about 3-4 in. across and is probably the most common coral inside the reef at Hanauma Bay. The branches are covered with wartlike bumps. In very calm environments branches become slender and delicate, hence the common name; in more turbulent areas, such as Hanauma, the branches are thicker and stubbier. Colonies are whitish to brown, depending on depth and available light (deeper colonies are darker). At Hanauma Bay isolated heads occur on the sides of the reef flat, or in depressions on the top. This almost ubiquitous Indo-Pacific and Eastern Pacific species was the first coral named by Linnaeus (in 1758) and is one of the most thoroughly studied corals in the world. It is often host to the Coral Gall Crab (*Hapalocarcinus marsupialis*), which creates and occupies hollow galls on the tips of branches. Galls (their openings resembling partly open mouths) can be seen on several of the lower branches of the colony shown here. Indo-Pacific and Eastern Pacific. Photo: Back Door Lagoon.

CAULIFLOWER CORAL • *Pocillopora meandrina*

This common coral forms compact branching colonies on hard substrate. Colonies are ordinarily light brown, but they can be green or rose-pink in very shallow water. (These pigments may help protect the coral from harmful ultraviolet radiation.) The flattened branches, usually equal in length, often curve into a "C" shape at the tips. Viewed from above, channels appear to meander between the branches, hence the species name. Crabs, shrimps, and fishes of several species commonly inhabit these spaces. This coral can occur anywhere from splash pools above high tide level to depths of 100 ft. or more. Thriving in high energy environments where few other Hawaiian corals (and no other branching ones) will live, it is typically the first coral to colonize new submarine lava flows. Colonies spawn synchronously between about 7:15 and 7:45 AM several days immediately following the first full moon after April 15. The milky gametes released often reduce visibility to a few feet. Heads attain a maximum diameter of about 18 in.; 12 in. is typical. At Hanauma a few colonies, such as the one shown here, grow inside the reef; outside the reef, of course, the species is abundant, especially along the sides of the bay on the left side. Photo: near Sandman's Patch.

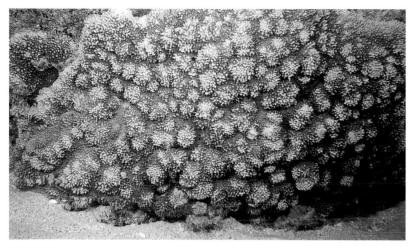

RICE CORAL • *Montipora capitata* •

This coral grows in a variety of forms but throughout Hanauma Bay it is typically encrusting. Its surface is studded with rounded projections like grains of rice set endwise. Color varies from dark brown to beige or cream, often with white edges or tips. In calm sheltered areas such as Kāne'ohe Bay, O'ahu, this species forms impressive colonies consisting of plates, cups, and delicate branching pinnacles. Colonies spawn simultaneously on the third night after the new moon in June and July, releasing little white bundles of eggs and sperm. Small patches of Rice Coral are common on vertical surfaces inside the reef at Hanauma Bay. Endemic to Hawai'i. Photo: Sandman's Patch.

BLUE RICE CORAL • *Montipora flabellata* •

The vivid fluorescent blue of this species makes it easy to identify, although in heavily shaded areas it may also be brown. The blue pigments appear pinkish under artificial strobe light, making realistic underwater photographs tricky to obtain. It encrusts rocky substrate in areas of strong water movement from the shallows down to about 20 ft. At Hanauma it is rare inside the reef but large encrusting patches are common on smooth rocky bottoms outside. Colonies can be 3 ft. across. Like most species of *Montipora*, the surface is rough and grainy due to small rounded projections between the calyces. The snapping shrimp *Alpheus deuteropus* sometimes inhabits this and other corals of the genera *Montipora* and *Porites,* creating dark branching channels on the surface. The species name is from *flabellum,* meaning "fan." Endemic to Hawai'i. Photo: Sandman's Patch.

SPREADING RICE CORAL • *Montipora patula* •
[SANDPAPER CORAL]

 The Latin word *patula,* meaning "spread out" or "broad," aptly describes this coral, which in Hanauma Bay typically grows in encrusting colonies often several feet or more across. The color varies from very light tan to brown. Its relatively small surface projections are of unequal height and tend to cluster around the widely spaced calyces. When open, the tiny polyps sometimes appear bright blue or violet. The species is fairly common inside the reef at Hanauma, where it grows on vertical surfaces. Endemic to Hawai'i. Photo: Back Door Lagoon.

PITTED CORAL • *Montipora incrassata*

 This coral forms irregular nodules covered with an irregular network of thick ridges, giving it a pitted appearance. At Hanauma Bay it is uncommon outside the reef and rare inside. In Hawai'i this coral was previously identified as *M. studeri.* The species name means "made thick." Indo-Pacific. Photo: Back Door Lagoon (with *Porites evermanni* above).

FINGER CORAL • **pōhaku puna** • *Porites compressa* ●

One of the two most abundant corals in Hawai'i (the other is Lobe Coral), Finger Coral forms extensive reefs in the outer half of Hanauma Bay, where it usually grows at depths below 40 ft. to avoid turbulence and surge. In localized calm areas of the bay, however, Finger Coral beds can be found as shallow as 10 ft. Inside the reef small stunted colonies, such as the one pictured here, are common along the seaward sides of the Back Door Lagoon. In deeper water, branches tend to be longer and more fingerlike. (See p.22) Colonies are usually light brown, sometimes yellowish or blue-gray. Finger Coral beds provide important habitat for juvenile fishes, and at night they come alive with colorful shrimps and other invertebrates. Endemic to Hawai'i. Photo: Back Door Lagoon.

EVERMANN'S CORAL • **pōhaku puna** • *Porites evermanni*

This coral forms medium-size, massive heads that vary from chocolate brown to bluish or purplish gray. It never has the yellowish or greenish color usually present in *P. lobata*. Heads can be 3 ft. or more across. Colony surfaces are typically crowded with many small rounded swellings or lobes. Often polyps are not completely retracted, giving the surface a slightly fuzzy appearance. Evermann's Coral is sometimes common on protected or semi-protected reef flats, but also occurs in deeper water. It is the most common massive coral inside the reef at Hanauma. A surprisingly large head grows close to shore in the Back Door Lagoon. The name honors American ichthyologist Barton Warren Evermann (1853-1932), who studied Hawaiian fishes in the early 20th century and later became director of San Francisco's Steinhart Aquarium. Formerly considered endemic to Hawai'i, this species is now known also from other parts of the Indo-Pacific. The Hawaiian population, however, differs in some details. Photo: Back Door Lagoon. (The light scrape marks on the surface are the work of grazing parrotfishes. The dark channels are created by Petroglyph Shrimps).

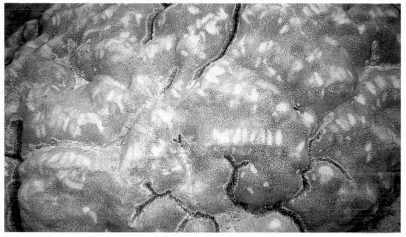

Lobe Coral (Back Door Lagoon). The scrape marks are made by parrotfishes.

Lobe Coral (typical head outside the reef) (D.R. & T.L. Schrichte)

LOBE CORAL · **pōhaku puna**
Porites lobata

This is Hawai'i's dominant coral. Colonies vary greatly in size and shape, depending largely on the amount of wave action. In shallow, turbulent areas they are encrusting; in calmer areas they form big hemispherical mounds—the typical form in Hanauma Bay. Large colonies in the bay are about 10 ft. across and perhaps 150 years old. Lobe Coral grows most profusely at depths between 15 and 30 ft. and is thus not abundant inside the reef. It varies from yellowish brown to yellowish green. Heads grow about 1/3 in. in diameter each year and are often deeply undercut at the base, providing shelter for fishes and invertebrates. The Petroglyph Shrimp (p.176) creates dark meandering channels on the surface of this and other corals. In Hanauma Bay, the greatest diversity of fishes and large invertebrates occurs where Lobe Coral is dominant. The species occurs throughout the Indo-Pacific. The numerous light scrape marks on the top photo are caused by grazing parrotfishes. The dark channels are the work of Petroglyph Shrimps.

DUERDEN'S CORAL • *Pavona duerdeni*
(PORKCHOP CORAL; FLAT LOBE CORAL)

Mature colonies of this coral form lobes flattened on two sides (often resembling porkchops, or thick upright disks partially buried). Young colonies are encrusting. Large lobes are about 12 in. high; entire colonies may attain diameters of 10 ft. or more. The tan surface is finely textured and smooth; the pattern formed by the calyces is particularly pleasing when viewed at close range. Somewhat stunted colonies of this coral are moderately common inside the reef at Hanauma Bay; outside the species occurs at depths of 20-30 ft. The name honors zoologist J.E. Duerden (1865-1937). Indo-Pacific. Photo: Back Door Lagoon.

CORRUGATED CORAL • *Pavona varians*

This coral usually forms encrusting patches that are light yellowish tan. Under shaded overhangs they may be brownish gray, greenish, or brown. In very protected areas it sometimes forms thin plates. Whatever its form or color, the calyces lie in meandering valleys separated by sharp narrow ridges. The species occurs from the surface to depths of at least 80 ft. Large colonies are about 8 in. across. Indo-Pacific. Photo: Sandman's Patch.

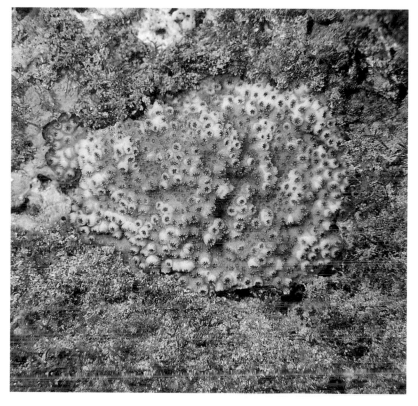

OCELLATED CORAL • *Cyphastrea ocellina*

This coral forms small encrusting, clumpy, or even knoblike hemispherical colonies. Encrusting colonies are 2 to 6 in. across, usually at depths of less than 25 ft., and are light reddish brown. The circular calyces (1/16 to 1/8 in. across) have sharply raised edges; they usually crowd together but nevertheless remain distinct. The species name means "little eyes." Indo-Pacific. Photo: Back Door Lagoon.

Zoanthids

Zoanthids, sometimes called colonial anemones, resemble stony corals but have no hard skeleton. Polyps are typically connected to their neighbors by common tissue containing channels that link their digestive cavities. Zoanthids generally occur in shallow water. Some overgrow exposed rock; others live partly buried in soft substrate. Like anemones and corals, they capture planktonic organisms with stinging tentacles and may also gain nourishment from sugars produced by symbiotic algae.

Zoanthid nematocysts are too weak to sting humans or deter predators. Their bodies and connective tissues, however, are often tough and leathery, and in many species are filled with embedded sand grains. Like anemones, zoanthids can close tightly when disturbed. As further protection, some contain a potent poison.

Aware of these toxic properties, Hawaiian warriors in the Hana district of Maui often smeared their spear tips with zoanthid mucus before battle. Wounds from such spears were usually fatal. Scientists believe the toxin to be a product not of the zoanthid itself, but of symbiotic algae or bacteria living in its tissues. Zoanthids from other parts of the world contain similar compounds. For this reason, it is best not to touch or handle zoanthids.

BLUE-GRAY ZOANTHID • *Palythoa caesia*
This common zoanthid forms tough mats on rocks and dead coral from the shallows to depths of about 25 ft. in areas of good water movement. The spaces between polyps are completely filled with connective tissue and sometimes sand. When the polyps close, the colony appears smooth and almost featureless. The overall color is typically light bluish gray, but pastel pinks and greens and various shades of brown are not unusual. At Hanauma Bay this zoanthid is abundant along much of the reef front. A few small colonies occur inside the reef. It might be toxic, so avoid contact with it. The species name means "blue-gray." Polyps are about 3/10 in. across. Indo-Pacific. Photo: Reef Face (Zone Two).

Jellyfishes

Free-swimming cnidarians are commonly called jellyfishes or sea jellies. Two distinct groups exist, true jellyfishes and box jellyfishes. (The word "jellyfish," however, is often loosely used for other gelatinous or floating animals such Portuguese Men-of-War or comb jellies, which are entirely different animals.) True jellyfishes are round, bell- or saucer-shape animals, usually with stinging tentacles. Box jellyfishes are similar but with a four-sided bell.

True jellyfishes are rarely encountered in Hawaiian waters except in quiet harbors where snorkelers rarely venture. Box jellyfishes are another matter, sometimes washing ashore on popular beaches by the hundreds. They have bells with four flattened sides and a long tentacle (or bundle of tentacles) attached to each of the four lower corners. Well-developed eyes (with lens and "retina") are present, and some species can swim up to 2 miles per hour. They generally prefer calm environments but also occur a mile or more offshore. Many can deliver a potent sting. The famous Sea Wasp *(Chironex fleckeri)*, a box jellyfish of northern Australia, can kill an adult human in as little as 3 minutes. Hawaiian box jellies are not as potent, but they deserve respect nonetheless. When these animals are sighted in Hanauma Bay, park authorities usually close the beach for the day.

Craig Thomas and Susan Scott, in their book *All Stings Considered*, offer the following first aid advice to beachgoers stung by a box jellyfish: 1) Flood the affected skin with vinegar to disable any undischarged nematocysts. (Do not use sand, fresh water, or anything else.) 2) If the eyes are stung, irrigate with fresh water for at least 15 minutes. Do not use vinegar in the eyes. 3) Remove any vinegar-soaked tentacles with a stick or other tool. 4) If the victim has breathing difficulties, weakness, palpitations, eye problems, or cramps seek emergency medical care. 5) If necessary, try either heat packs or ice packs for pain relief. (Most stings subside by themselves within an hour.)

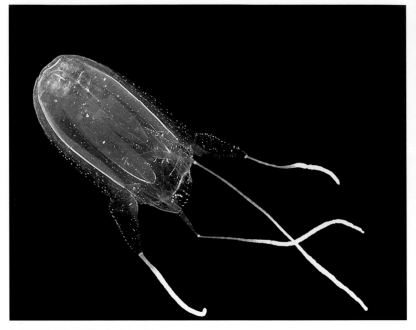

WINGED BOX JELLYFISH • *Carybdea alata*

Colorless and transparent, these jellies have elongated bells up to about 3 in. high and 2 in. wide. Outside Hawai'i they may be 10 in. high. Four tentacles up to 2 ft. long hang from the edge of the bell, one from each corner. In the water these animals resemble floating plastic bags and are difficult to see. Normally they live at depths of 10-60 ft. on the leeward sides of the islands, some distance from shore. Eight to ten nights after a full moon, however, they move into shallow water to reproduce, swimming up to two miles per hour. Attracted to light, hundreds or thousands can wash up during a single night, plagueing south-facing beaches. Contact with their tentacles or any part of the animal creates an immediate and intense burning sensation equal to or exceeding that of the Portuguese Man-of-War (a colonial hydroid, not a jellyfish). The pain usually subsides by itself in less than one hour but can linger as long as eight. Skin irritation may persist for weeks or months. If weakness, cramps, or breathing difficulties occur the victim should seek emergency medical treatment. (For first-aid see the section above.) The species name means "winged." These animals occur in warm seas around the world. Photo: David B. Fleetham. Molokini Islet, Maui.

Crustaceans
Phylum Arthropoda • Subphylum Crustacea

The crustaceans are a subgroup within the vast assemblage of animals with jointed appendages called arthropods—the largest single group of animals on earth. Probably over a million species of arthropods exist, most of them insects. Like insects on land, crustaceans are ubiquitous in the aquatic realm, having penetrated all ocean, river, lake, and stream habitats. Most are small or microscopic organisms, but about one third belong to the order Decapoda, which includes the familiar lobsters, shrimps, and crabs.

Crustaceans (and arthropods in general) boast an amazing variety of jointed appendages used not only to move about and capture food, but also to eat, breathe, sense the environment, and reproduce. They are also characterized by an exterior skeleton, or shell, composed of plates and rings of a flexible, horny substance called chitin. In the larger crustaceans this shell is often calcified, making it thick and hard. The shell provides protection and a rigid framework to which muscles attach, but it must be shed periodically to allow for the animal's growth.

Most crustaceans are active only at night and thus are seldom found by snorkelers. Except for the Petroglyph Shrimp, the species below can be seen by day at Hanauma Bay.

Shrimps

Shrimps are decapods (ten-legged crustaceans) with cylindrical carapaces and long muscular tails ending in a tail fan, or telson. Their shells are thin, flexible, and never calcified like those of some crabs and lobsters. Most have pincers on their first two or three pairs of legs, whiplike antennae, and a rostrum—a prolongation of the carapace between the eyes that is often sharply pointed. When threatened, most shrimps can shoot backwards by rapidly flexing their powerful tails.

Large shrimps (often called prawns) attain a length of about 8 in. Small species are less than 1/4 in. long. The average size is from 1 to 3 in. The general name for shrimps in Hawaiian is ʻōpae. As well as eating them, ancient Hawaiians used shrimps in sorcery to cast out evil spirits. The term poʻo ʻōpae ("shrimp head") was an insult.

Shrimps are rarely seen by snorkelers in Hanauma Bay, but evidence of their presence is common. The dark branching channels common in many living corals are created by Petroglyph Shrimps (below), and most of the holes in the sandy bottoms of the lagoons are probably made either by lobsterlike, nocturnal ghost shrimps (family Callianassidae) or by goby-associated snapping shrimps.

BANDED CORAL SHRIMP • *Stenopus hispidus*

These striking red and white shrimps, also known as Barber Pole Shrimps, typically cling upside down to the undersides of ledges and coral heads, almost always in pairs. They can usually be spotted by their prominent white antennae, which signal their presence to other reef-dwellers. These shrimps will clean eels or other fishes, although in Hawai'i they are rarely seen doing so, perhaps because they are most active at night. Females are slightly larger than males and frequently carry a light greenish blue egg mass under their abdomens. The species name means "bristly" or "spiny" because the upper surfaces of the body and legs are covered with small hooked spines, forward-pointing at the front of the body, backward-pointing at the rear. This colorful species occurs in all warm seas, from tide pools to depths of 100 ft. or more, attaining about 2 in. body length. Photo: Lāna'i Lookout, O'ahu.

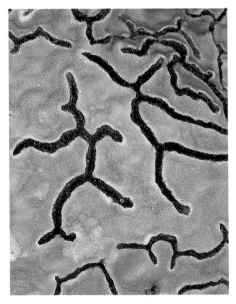

PETROGLYPH SHRIMP • *Alpheus deuteropus*

Although these little snapping shrimps are never seen, their presence is evident on virtually any Hawaiian reef. Pairs create and inhabit the conspicuous dark fissures or channels common on the surface of massive or encrusting corals, usually Lobe Coral. They also live in Evermann's Coral, Rice Coral, Blue Rice Coral, Spreading Coral, and others. Their channels, up to about 10 in. long and often branched, are sometimes reminiscent of ancient Hawaiian petroglyphs. The shrimps, which "farm" filamentous algae in the channels, live in burrows deep inside, usually in mated pairs. They are laterally compressed and mostly colorless with scattered red spots on the carapace. They may excavate the coral by chemical means. Indo-Pacific. To about 1 1/4 in. Photo: Ali'i Beach Park, O'ahu (in Lobe Coral).

Hermit Crabs

Anyone who has explored Hawai'i's tide pools is familiar with the hermits, the little crabs that live in snail shells. Although their front parts are covered by an external skeleton like other crabs, their long soft tails (abdomens) are typically unprotected. For this reason, most hermit crabs occupy an empty snail shell, coiling their tails deep inside and holding on from within with the help of their tiny, specialized last pair of legs. Not only is the tail protected by this arrangement, the entire animal can withdraw into the shell when threatened. It may seal the shell's opening from the inside with an oversize claw, or retreat so far that no body part is visible. The general Hawaiian name for hermit crabs is **unauna**.

ELEGANT HERMIT CRAB • *Calcinus elegans*
At Hanauma Bay this colorful hermit is sometimes found crawling along the top of the reef, where it can easily be seen by sharp-eyed snorkelers. It also occurs to depths of at least 30 ft. Larger individuals are usually found at the deeper end of the range. The walking legs are dark brown with bright orange bands, and the last segments are bright orange with black spots. (Orange coloration occurs only in Hawaiian specimens. Elsewhere in the Indo-Pacific the bands are turquoise blue.) The two almost equal-size claws are brownish speckled with white and have white tips. The eyes and eyestalks are bright blue, the antennae orange, the back white. The maximum carapace length is about 3/4 in. Indo-Pacific. Photo: Hekili Point, Maui. (in triton shell).

SEURAT'S HERMIT CRAB • *Calcinus seurati*

These gregarious hermit crabs live in rocky pools of the splash zone just above sea level among the periwinkles and nerites, whose empty shells they usually occupy. Look for them as you walk to the Toilet Bowl or to Witch's Brew Point. They can tolerate warm stagnant water and will sometimes crawl about above the waterline on wet, algae-covered rock. Bold black and white bands on the legs make them obvious as they move. The claws are gray. The left claw, much larger than the right, blocks the entrance to the shell when the crab withdraws. The eyes are bright blue, the eyestalks orange. These hermits are most common along shores where the sea is rough and waves splash high. They are named for Gaston Seurat, who first collected them in French Polynesia between 1901 and 1905. To about 1/4 in. carapace length. Indo-Pacific. Photo: Makapu'u, O'ahu. Tide pool.

True Crabs

True crabs—as opposed to hermit crabs and their allies—are the typical crabs of the seashore. Their broad, flattened carapaces and sideways scuttle are familiar to most beachgoers. They have an enlarged first pair of pincer-bearing limbs and, usually, four pairs of walking legs. Their abbreviated tails are carried tucked under their bodies, giving many of them an agility that long-tailed shrimps and lobsters cannot match, and their flattened compact bodies fit easily into small crevices and under stones. Crabs may be predators, scavengers, or algae-eaters. Most are marine; some inhabit fresh water. A few spend their adult lives on dry land, returning to the water only to spawn.

In Hanauma Bay small crabs are common under stones in shallow water but are not ordinarily seen. Larger ones live on rocks along the shoreline. The conical piles of sand on the beach, usually seen in the early morning when the tide is low, are made by male Horn-Eyed Ghost Crabs to attract females. The higher the pile, the more desirable its owner. The general name for crabs in Hawaiian is **pāpaʻi**, but many groups had special names, such as **pokipoki** (box crabs).

SEVEN-ELEVEN CRAB · ʻalakuma · *Carpilius maculatus*
Because of its large size and unmistakable color pattern, this is one of the best known Indo-Pacific reef crabs. Slow-moving and nocturnal, it is usually seen resting quietly in a crevice by day. The massive claw-bearing limbs are of unequal size; the smooth, heavy shell lacks spines. It has seven prominent red spots (two by each eye, three in the center) and four less obvious ones (along the rear margin), making a total of eleven spots. In old Hawaiʻi the story was told of a hungry god who caught an **ʻalakuma**. The frantic crab pinched its captor and drew blood, escaping with bloody marks on its back. Again the god grabbed the crab; again the crab pinched and got free. The third time the god was successful, but to this day the crab's descendants bear his bloody finger prints. This crab has been observed carrying urchins and cowries, suggesting a possible food preference. The species name means "spotted." To about 6 in. carapace width. Indo-Pacific. Photo: Pūpūkea, Oʻahu.

LUMPY BOX CRAB • **pokipoki** • *Calappa gallus*

This slow-moving crab resembles a lumpy rock. It prefers rubble environments where its rough, knobby carapace (sometimes with bits of algae growing on it) blends perfectly with the surroundings. Sensing danger it freezes, folding its heavy knobbed claws almost seamlessly against its body. Some specimens, like the one pictured, have a large black spot on either side of the carapace. The orangish legs, although usually out of sight under the winglike extensions of the carapace, are visible when the crab moves. This species sometimes occurs intertidally. It can partially bury itself but probably spends most of its time on the surface. The species name means "rooster," perhaps because the row of heavy spines on the upper edge of each claw resembles a cockscomb. To about 2 1/2 in. carapace width. Indo-Pacific. Photo: Swimming Area.

THIN-SHELLED ROCK CRAB • **'a'ama** • *Grapsus tenuicrustatus*

These crabs (often called "Sally Lightfoot Crabs") are ubiquitous on rocky shores, clambering about in the splash zone and retreating into crevices or the water when approached. Look for them on the boulders at the left end of the beach and along the sides of the bay. They are greenish black, marked with faint striations. Their molted shells, found high on the rocks, often turn bright red from the heat of the sun (just as a lobster turns red when boiled). Edible, they were of importance in old Hawai'i and gave rise to a number of stories and sayings. When trouble arose and people gathered out of curiosity, people said "When the sea is rough the **'a'ama** crabs climb up on the rocks." The Hawaiian name means "to loosen or relax." To ask a favor of the gods, an **'a'ama** might be offered, that the gods would "loosen" and grant it. The species name means "thin shell." To about 3 in. carapace width. Indo-Pacific. Photo: Waikīkī, O'ahu.

Barnacles

Barnacles are strangely modified crustaceans that spend their adult lives attached permanently to rocks, pilings, floating objects or other animals. They feed by rhythmically sweeping the water with featherlike jointed appendages (cirri) to collect drifting food particles. When active, barnacles extend their cirri through an opening in the shell. When resting, exposed at low tide, or disturbed they draw in their cirri and seal their "houses," usually with two pairs of hinged plates. Roughly 50 barnacle species occur in Hawaiʻi, many brought here on ships from other parts of the world. The Hawaiian word for barnacles is **pīʻoeʻoe**. In old Hawaiʻi, persons constantly pursued by the opposite sex were described as "clung to by barnacles." Europeans have similar ideas. In 1904, when Irish writer James Joyce first dated his wife-to-be, Nora Barnacle, his father predicted "She'll never leave him."

PURPLE ROCK BARNACLES · **piʻoeʻoe** · *Nesochthamalus intertextus*
These small purplish or whitish barnacles cluster along semi-exposed rocky shores where they are submerged only at high tide or by periodic surge. At Hanauma Bay you can find them along the ledges at the sides of the bay, especially on the left side as you walk to the Toilet Bowl. The species was first described by the great naturalist Charles Darwin (1809-1882). Although better known for his theory of evolution, Darwin was also an ardent student of barnacles. The species name means "interwoven." Typically about 1/4 in. across the base. Indo-Pacific. Photo: Lānaʻi Lookout, Oʻahu.

Echinoderms (Phylum Echinodermata)

This group of unusual marine animals includes the sea stars (starfish), brittle stars, sea cucumbers, and sea urchins. No other animals are built like them. The name comes from Greek words for "spiny skin," but perhaps the most unusual characteristic of these animals is their five-part body plan, with circulatory, nervous, and skeletal systems radiating in five directions from a central axis. Head, brain, and heart are absent. Of the major body systems, only the digestive system is not radial. The mouth and anus generally lie at opposite ends of the body's central axis, on the lower and upper surfaces, respectively (or in sea cucumbers, at the ends); the digestive tract runs between them.

Echinoderms have an internal calcareous skeleton. Actually, it is the skeleton, not the skin, that bears the spines for which echinoderms are named. In some echinoderms, such as sea urchins, the skeleton is fairly obvious; in others it takes the form of disconnected plates or even microscopic ossicles radially arranged within the skin or flesh.

Many echinoderms are either scavengers or predators on stationary (sessile) organisms such as algae, corals, sponges, clams, and oysters. Others filter food particles from sand, mud, or water. Echinoderms are exclusively marine, ranging from brackish intertidal zones to abyssal depths. Of about 6,500 living species, some 280 occur in Hawaiian waters. Echinoderms vary in size from tiny urchins and stars about 1 in. across to sea cucumbers 6 ft. long; most are in the 4 to 5 in. range. Sea stars do not ordinarily occur inside the reef at Hanauma, but sea cucumbers and sea urchins are common. Brittle stars are also common, but stay mostly hidden during the day.

Sea Urchins

These animals are characterized by a globular skeleton (test) bristling with hundreds of movable spines. Numerous tube feet tipped with suckers help them to cling or move about. Sea urchin spines can be long, short, slender, stubby, or clublike. Members of the large tropical family Diadematidae have exceptionally long, sharp, sometimes venomous spines. Puncture wounds from long-spined urchins can be intensely painful. In Hawai'i, fortunately, these urchins are not common in shallow water.

How did sea urchins get their name? Although an urchin today is "a small, mischievous boy," in old England the word meant "hedgehog." The ancient Hawaiians had distinct names for at least four categories of urchins: **wana** (those with long slender spines), **'ina** (medium-length slender spines), **hāwa'e** (short slender spines) and **hā'uke'uke** (thick, flattened or stubby spines). They considered the gonads of many urchins a delicacy, eating them raw, cooked, or dried, and also prepared sauces and condiments using the urchin's inner liquids. Certain Hawaiian families and individuals, however, revered **wana** as **'aumakua** (the embodiment of ancestors). Such people neither harmed nor ate urchins; an urchin appearing in a dream or vision was held by them to have special meaning.

About 22 urchin species are known from shallow Hawaiian waters. Below are the three most commonly seen in Hanauma Bay; the observant snorkeler will also find others.

Hanauma Bay's rocky sides are riddled with small pits and channels excavated by Rock-Boring Urchins. Helmet Urchins are common here too. Red Pencil Urchins are seen in this environment rarely and only during very low tides.

BANDED URCHIN • **wana** • *Echinothrix calamaris*

Although Hawai'i's most common long-spined urchin, this species is encountered more often by divers than by snorkelers. It has hollow, slender, needle-like spines that often wave menacingly upon a close approach. The spines are usually dull black but may be banded or even grayish white. Hollow and fragile, they are easily broken. Younger urchins have banded white and dark green spines. Punctures can be intensely painful and may become purplish black from a dye in the spines, but they are not ordinarily dangerous. In most cases the pain subsides in an hour or so and the body absorbs the spines within 24 hours to 3 weeks. Joints close to punctures may ache for weeks, however. Fortunately, these urchins seldom occur in the shallow snorkeling areas of Hanauma Bay. They grow to about 8 in. across, including the spines. Indo-Pacific. Photo: Witch's Brew area (Zone 2).

HELMET URCHIN • **hāʻukeʻuke kaupali** • *Colobocentrotus atratus*
[SHINGLE URCHIN; ARMORED URCHIN]

These unusual urchins cling to exposed rocky shores where few other animals survive. Their domed tests are covered with stubby, shingle-like spines that offer little resistance to the surf. Longer flat spines ring the test like a skirt of armor. Covered with water they are deep purple; exposed to air they are almost black. Despite the constant pounding of enormous waves, they creep about almost imperceptibly on their strong tube feet, scraping thin films of algae from the rocks. At low tide on calm days look for them from shore as you walk around to the Toilet Bowl; admire from a distance; sudden large waves can be dangerous. The Hawaiian name **kaupali** means "cliff-clinging." The species name means "dressed in black" (as if in mourning). In old Hawai'i it was said "When the **hala** fruit ripens, the **hāʻukeʻuke** is fat," meaning that the tests are full of eggs or sperm and ready to eat. To about 3 in. Indo-Pacific. Photo: Makapu'u, O'ahu.

ROCK-BORING URCHIN • 'ina kea •
Echinometra mathaei

This is the most common urchin in Hawai'i and possibly the entire Indo-Pacific. By continually scraping with its short spines and five-toothed mouth it is able to excavate into solid basalt rock. Most shallow reef flats in Hawai'i are riddled with channels and holes bored by these animals over the years. Its color ranges from greenish white to reddish and it is abundant in holes on the reef flat at Hanauma Bay. Similar black urchins occurring in the same shallow habitat are a different species, *E. oblonga.* Because these urchins stay in their holes, punctures from their spines are rare. In Hawaiian, **'ina** denotes an urchin with medium-length spines, and **kea** means "white." Reddish specimens were called **'ina 'ula.** To about 2 1/2 in., including the spines. Indo-Pacific. Photo: Swimming Area.

RED PENCIL URCHIN • hā'uke'uke 'ula'ula •
Heterocentrotus mammillatus
[SLATE PENCIL URCHIN]

These striking urchins have bright red, clublike spines that add a characteristic color note to many Hawaiian reefs. The shorter stubby spines covering the test vary from almost white to very dark red. A thin layer of live tissue covering the spines inhibits the growth of algae and other marine organisms. Years ago, when blackboards were made of slate, the long spines could be used in place of chalk, thus the alternate common name Slate Pencil Urchin. In old Hawai'i the spines were decoratively carved. The Hawaiian name **'ula'ula** means red. Another Hawaiian name is **pūnohu.** The species name means "having breasts" or "nipples," referring to the nodules prominent on the tests of dead specimens. In Hanauma Bay these are generally seen only outside the reef. They seldom exceed 8 in., including the spines. The species occurs throughout the Indo-Pacific but is abundant only in Hawai'i. Photo: Witch's Brew area.

Sea Cucumbers

These animals are common in Hanauma Bay, clinging to rocky reefs or lying like big sausages on the sand. Many smaller species live hidden lives beneath stones, in crevices, or partially buried in sand.

Most large cucumbers feed by slowly sweeping their down-turned mouth back and forth across the bottom. Swallowing sand, sediment, or mud, they filter out the organic matter and excrete the remainder in strands or piles of pellets. Some cucumbers use their tentacles to catch organic matter suspended in the water. When molested some species of sea cucumbers expel remarkably sticky white threads from their anus to entangle and confuse predators. Others expel their internal organs. Many are poisonous when eaten.

In the Hawaiian language, sea cucumbers are known as **loli**. In olden days many kinds were recognized and named, but we no longer know to which species all the names apply. Some **loli** were eaten and others perhaps used as medicine. Sea cucumbers were also used in love magic. "When **loli** is the offering," it was said, "passionate is the love."

Two species commonly seen by snorkelers are illustrated below. A few smaller species also occur inside the reef, usually under stones.

WHITE-SPOTTED SEA CUCUMBER • loli • *Actinopyga mauritiana*
These cucumbers cling tightly to vertical surfaces in areas of strong surge where other species might be swept away. Snorkelers at Hanauma Bay can almost always find them attached to boulders on the seaward side of the reef. They also occur inside. To about 8 in. Indo-Pacific. Photo: Keyhole Lagoon.

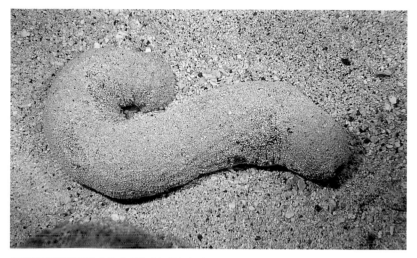

BLACK SEA CUCUMBER · **loli okuhi kuhi** · *Holothuria atra*

This is Hawai'i's most common large sea cucumber. It lies fully exposed on sand or rubble bottoms from the shallows to depths of at least 100 ft., its smooth black surface usually coated with a fine layer of sand. (Sometimes circular sandless "holes" occur in pairs along the sides.) A small commensal crab, *Lissocarcinus orbicularis*, often inhabits the tentacles and mouth. Although this sea cucumber is eaten and has commercial value in some parts of Asia, it is toxic unless properly prepared. The species name means "black." To about 20 in. Indo-Pacific.

TEATED SEA CUCUMBER · **loli** · *Holothuria whitmaei*

This cucumber is less common inside the reef at Hanauma Bay than the species above, which it resembles. Its black surface is usually coated with fine sand and is rock hard to the touch. Teat like projections along its base give it its name. To about 12 in. Indo-Pacific. Photo: Zone Three.

Molluscs · Phylum Mollusca

Molluscs (also spelled "mollusks") are soft, legless animals that usually secrete a calcium carbonate shell. ("Molluscus" means "soft" in Latin.) Clams, snails, slugs, squids, and octopuses belong to this group. With 85,000 to 110,000 species (estimates vary), molluscs are by far the largest group of animals in the sea, and many others live on land. People are generally more familiar with mollusc shells than with the animals themselves. Throughout history, mollusc shells have been used for ornaments, tools, and even money. Some molluscs, however, have internal shells (squids, cuttlefishes, and many slugs) or no shells at all (octopuses and nudibranchs). The animals themselves are evolutionarily advanced, with well-defined organs and complex sensory, circulatory, digestive, and reproductive systems. A few approach mammals in intelligence.

About 1,650 species of molluscs are known from Hawai'i, of which approximately half are marine. Of these, snails and slugs are the largest group, followed by bivalves (clams and oysters). Many of these animals live under sand, hide in crevices during the day, or are extremely well camouflaged, thus snorkelers see them only occasionally. Some octopuses and squids, however, are active by day and quite noticeable due to their large size.

BLACK NERITE · **pipipi** · *Nerita picea*
These snails are abundant on rocky shores in the splash zone above the waterline (but below the zone occupied by periwinkles). By day, dozens can often be found clustering under ledges and in crevices well out of the water. At night they graze more actively. They are black with fine spiral lines. The species name means "pitch black." To about 1/2 in. Possibly endemic. Photo: Moku'auia (Island), O'ahu.

DOTTED PERIWINKLE • **pipipi kōlea** • *Littoraria pintado*
       The largest of three common periwinkles in Hawai'i, Dotted Periwinkles are purple-gray, dotted with brown or black. They are abundant in the splash zone on most rocky shores just above the nerites, where waves only occasionally wet them. At low tide or when seas are calm they seal themselves tightly to prevent desiccation, remaining stuck to the rocks with a film of dried mucus. C.H. Edmondson of the Bishop Museum once wrote: "In my laboratory a periwinkle once climbed high up on the wall and stuck there. After almost a year, when taken down and wet with sea water, it promptly became active again." The species name means "painted" or "mottled" in Spanish. The Hawaiian name refers to the **kolea**, or Pacific Golden Plover, a migratory bird with mottled plumage that winters in Hawai'i. East Africa to Clipperton Atoll (Eastern Pacific). To almost 1 in. Photo: Lāi'e Point, O'ahu

SPOTTED DRUPE • **makaloa** • *Drupa ricina*
       Drupes live openly on the reef, their thick, encrusted shells resembling lumps on the rocky substrate. This species has a whitish shell with four rows of black tubercles that create a spotted appearance, but in shallow water coralline algae growing on the shell usually obscures the black markings. The outer lip bears five spines. The living animal is green and white. Perhaps Linnaeus thought the black tubercles resembed ticks, for that is one meaning of the Latin species name. To about 1 1/4 in. Indo-Pacific. Photo: Back Door Lagoon.

ARMORED DYE SHELL • *Thais armigera*
These large drupes have thick, spindle-shape shells covered by blunt tubercles. The aperture is yellowish brown. Common along some exposed rocky coasts at depths of 2-40 ft., the shells are typically covered with reddish coralline algae. They often occur in pairs. The species name means "bearing arms." To about 3 in. Indo-Pacific. Photo: Toilet Bowl.

CONE SHELL • **pupu 'ala** • *Conus* sp.
The cones form one of the largest families of marine snails. Their smooth, usually heavy shells are often beautifully patterned. In shallow water, however, they are typically covered by coralline algae and other growths, which make identification difficult. Like many molluscs, cone snails are most active at night. By day they either withdraw completely into their shells (which lie inert on the reef) or bury themselves in sand or rubble. Cone shells can sting; it's best not to handle them. Cone shells that live inside the reef at Hanauma Bay are typically 1-2 in. long. This one is probably the Yellow Cone (*Conus flavidus*), one of the most abundant cones on O'ahu's shallow reefs. Photo: Swimming Area.

CLUMPY NUDIBRANCH • *Asteronotus cespitosus*

This large, shallow-water sea slug occurs both on rocky substrate and on sand. Unlike many of its kind it is active by day, and at Hanauma Bay it is typically seen crawling across the rubble or reef top in broad daylight. Yellowish, gray-brown, or greenish, the surface of its firm rounded body is studded with irregular warts or bumps. (A 19th century zoologist, who was also a medical doctor, once compared its appearance to "a horrid disease.") Lacking the protection of an external shell, most sea slugs are poisonous or distasteful to predators. The species name means "turf-colored" or "clumpy." To about 5 in. Indo-Pacific. Photo: Swimming Area.

Day Octopus (see next page). The deep reddish brown color shows that the animal is alarmed at the approach of the photographer

Day Octopus—Puckered, camouflaged appearance.

DAY OCTOPUS • **he'e mauli** • *Octopus cyanea*

This is the most frequently seen Hawaiian octopus. Active by day, especially during the early morning and late afternoon, it occurs from the shallows to depths of 150 ft. or more. Snorkelers usually see it peering from its lair or scuttling over the reef in search of food. Like most octopuses it can assume a variety of color patterns and skin textures both as camouflage and to communicate its "emotional" state. Grayish brown is normal, but a startled octopus may flush deep reddish brown, and an aggressive or threatened one bleaches to ashen white with a dark circle (ocellus) on each side. A hiding octopus can adopt a range of mottled patterns matching the color of almost any background; its skin may pucker into complex bumps, warts, and ridges, merging with the texture of the reef. If detected, it jets away, often changing color several times to confuse the predator. Even while resting, subtle colors play almost continually along the body of this amazing animal.

The Day Octopus is solitary and spends much of its time half emerged from its lair, often surrounded by scattered fragments of crustacean shells. If approached it withdraws but almost always emerges in a minute or two to look at a snorkeler who waits quietly nearby. If attacked in its hole it squirts a powerful current of water at the intruder through its funnel. If that fails, it wraps itself in its arms, suckers out, or uses its suckers to pull a wall of stones between it and its attacker. At night it barricades itself in its hole with stones in a similar manner. Only as a last resort, or when suddenly surprised, does it eject its ink.

This species eats mostly crabs. Like most octopuses, it captures a prey animal by pouncing on it with the web between its arms spread wide, thus enclosing it. The octopus may inject a dose of poisonous saliva to weaken or kill the animal before it is consumed. Tough shells are no barrier; the octopus can drill straight through with a rasplike organ called the radula. Octopuses are strongly attracted to certain cowries, which were used in old times as lures. (In those days, when a man looked lecherously at young girls, it was said "the octopus notices the little cowries.")

Octopus cyanea is widespread in the Indo-Pacific. It attains about 3 ft. with arms spread, with a weight of 4-5 pounds. Like many cephalopods, its life span is only about a year. It was named for Cyane, a nymph in Greek mythology who was turned into a fountain. Photos: p.191—Palea Point (Zone Three); this page—Pūpūkea, O'ahu.

◄────── see also previous page.

OVAL SQUID • **mūhe'e** • *Sepioteuthis lessoniana*

Squids in Hawai'i are typically schooling, open-water animals not found close to coral reefs. Sightings were rare until the spring and summer of 2001 when small groups of Oval Squids appeared in shallow water in Hanauma Bay and elsewhere off O'ahu. (No one could predict whether they would stay, or disappear again for years.) Like all squids, these have eight arms and two longer tentacles, used to capture prey. This particular genus is characterized by two expanded fins forming an oval and extending almost the length of the mantle. By rippling these fins the squid can swim forward or backward; for speed it jets backward. (In old Hawai'i it was said that the squid "moves two ways, like a crab.") These animals can change color in an instant as various iridescent hues ripple down their bodies. Beautiful rows of spots sometimes appear along the margins of the fins. This species is of commercial importance; in Japan it has been found to mature in fewer than 100 days, females growing to about 10 in., males to about 14 in. It has a life span of 9-10 months and is one of the few squids that have been successfully maintained in captivity. Eastern Indian Ocean to Hawai'i. Photo: just outside the Telephone Cable Channel (Zone Two).

Worms

Legless invertebrates with slender or flattened bodies are commonly called worms. Animals of many phyla fit this description. Most live their lives hidden in sand or mud, under stones, in crevices, or as parasites or symbionts of larger animals. Few are ever seen by snorkelers, and those that are may not resemble our usual idea of a worm at all. The animal below belongs to a group called the annelid worms (phylum Annelida). It is distantly related to the common earthworm.

SPAGHETTI WORM • **kauna'oa** • *Loimia medusa*

Bluish white tentacles strung haphazardly over the rocks and rubble indicate the presence of a Spaghetti Worm buried nearby. Like most tube-dwelling worms, its body (encased in a tough buried tube covered with bits of shell and gravel) is never seen. Food particles adhering to the sticky strands are either passed to the worm's mouth through grooves extending the length of the tentacle, or the tentacle contracts toward the mouth dragging the particles with it. The soft, conspicuous tentacles are possibly protected by a poison. (Spaghetti worms were used medicinally in old Hawai'i and their tentacles contain anticancer compounds.) This animal occurs worldwide in warm seas. Its unseen body can be almost 12 in. long, with tentacles at least twice that length. Photo: Swimming Area.

Coralline Algae

Some marine plants—notably species of red algae (Rhodophyta)—deposit calcium carbonate in their cell walls as they grow. This is limestone, the same substance secreted by stony corals. Like cnidarian corals, some of these plants become hard and stony. Known as crustose coralline algae, they play an important role in the building of coral reefs, cementing together sediment and coral rubble, overgrowing dead coral, and laying down significant quantities of limestone in their own right. Much, perhaps most, of the "coral limestone" in Hawai'i and elsewhere is actually a product of these plants. For this reason some scientists prefer the term "biotic reefs" in place of "coral reefs."

Many species of coralline algae thrive in shallow water along rocky turbulent shores where cnidarian corals cannot easily grow. They form hard rocky sheets over the substrate, which over time accumulate into a tough pavement of limestone highly resistant to the impact of waves. This is particularly true at the outer edge of reefs where turbulence is constant. Here they form a slightly elevated "algal ridge," which is typically exposed at low tide and which protects the inner reef flat from strong wave action. The outer edge of the fringing reef at Hanauma is a good example of an algal ridge. (See page 7.) In fact, Hanauma's entire fringing reef appears to be primarily algal, although built on an underlying foundation of true coral.

Some species of coralline algae form pink, tan, or purplish crusts on the rocks; others form leafy plates or branching structures somewhat similar to those created by cnidarian corals. Coralline algae of one sort or another will grow on almost any object in Hawai'i's shallow seas, be it natural or artificial, and can cover close to 100 percent of the bottom. Much of the loose rubble resulting from the blasting in Hanauma Bay in 1956 and later, for example, is now covered with smooth encrustations of reddish or bluish coralline algae. Eventually, the algae may cement these nodules together. Another form of reef-building by coralline algae occurs in Hanauma Bay wherever heads of Cauliflower Coral are common. When such a colony dies, coralline algae (probably *Hydrolithon onkodes*) soon begin overgrowing the dead skeleton, eventually filling in the spaces between the branches and turning the once living coral colony into just another rocky lump on the reef. All stages of overgrowth are easy to find in Zone 2.

Four species of coralline algae common in Hanauma Bay are shown below. *Hydrolithon onkodes,* mentioned above, is the most important reef-builder. Hawai'i's coralline algae are poorly known, however, and the identifications given here are only tentative. Note that coralline algae never have calyces or polyps like true corals.

Hydrolithon reinboldi forms lumpy bluish or lavender encrustations on rubble or dead coral. It often forms loose nodules that roll with the surf and is found mainly on reef flats in shallow water but also down to at least 60 ft. Photo: Swimming Area.

Sporolithon erythraea is similar to the species above but forms smooth reddish or greenish encrustations. It is abundant in the Swimming Area inside the reef at Hanauma where it encrusts rubble created by past blasting. Given time, it will probably cement the separate pieces together into solid limestone.

Hydrolithon gardineri forms both encrustations and masses of knobs and slender branches, which may be round or flattened in cross-section. Common on shallow reef flats where there is strong water movement, it is usually pale pinkish or greenish. Heads can be 1 ft. or more across but inside the reef at Hanauma they are usually small and poorly developed. Photo: Waialua, Oʻahu.

Coralline algae overgrowing dead Cauliflower Coral at Palea Point (Zone Three). See next page.

Coralline algae, probably *Hydrolithon onkodes,* overgrowing a dead colony of Cauliflower Coral. After filling in the spaces between the branches, the limestone-depositing plant—visible only as a rocky crust—will completely overgrow the old coral colony, transforming it into just another rocky lump on the reef. All stages of this process can easily be seen in shallow water outside the reef in Hanauma Bay. The Greek species name, meaning "bulk" or "mass" or "weight," is appropriate; this plant has deposited much, perhaps most, of the "coral limestone" in Hawai'i and other Indo-Pacific locations. The species was formerly placed in the genus *Porolithon.* Photo: Pūpūkea, O'ahu.

⟵ see also previous page.

BIBLIOGRAPHY

The following articles, books, and websites were used in the preparation of this book. They are organized by subject.

History

Anon, 1956. **Cable project blasting ousts Hanauma swimmers.** Honolulu Advertiser Oct. 13, 1956. A1-1.

Benson, Bruce, 1970. **Dike planned at Hanauma.** Honolulu Advertiser, April 29, 1970. E1-3.

Brock, Richard E. & Alan Kam, 2000. **Carrying capacity study for the Hanauma Bay Nature Preserve final report** (contract 69919) prepared for: Department of Parks and Recreation, City and County of Honolulu, 650 South King Street, 10th Floor, Honolulu, Hawaii 96813.

Clark, John R.K., 1977. **The Beaches of O'ahu.** Honolulu, University Press of Hawaii. 193 p. (Clark's definitive books on the beaches of each island are rich in historical details as well as practical information.)

Coral Reef Assessment and Management Program. **Hanauma Bay CRAMP Site** http://cramp.wcc.hawaii.edu/Study_Sites/Oahu/Hanauma_Bay/ Accessed June, 2001 (Lots of aerial photographs and an informative time line.)

Easton, W.H. & E.A. Olson, 1976. **Radiocarbon profile of Hanauma Reef, Oahu, Hawaii.** Geological Society of America Bulletin 87: 711-719.

Grigg, Richard W., 1998. **Holocene coral reef accretion in Hawaii, a function of wave exposure and sea level history.** Coral Reefs 17: 263-272.

Grossman, Eric E. & Charles H. Fletcher, III, 1998. **Sea level higher than present 3500 years ago on the northern main Hawaiian Islands.** Geology 26(4): 363-366.

The Hawaiian Language Website. Hawaiian Language Pronunciation: A List of Common Mispronunciations. http://www.geocities.com/~olelo/wl-mispronunciations.html#TOP Accessed June, 2001

Honolulu (Hawaii). Dept. of Design and Construction, 1999. **Final environmental impact statement : improvements to Hanauma Bay Nature Preserve,** Koko Head Regional Park & Nature Preserve, **East Honolulu, Island of Oahu.** [Honolulu : The Dept.] 1 v.

Hostetler, Harold, 1970. **Officials blame phone cables.** Honolulu Advertiser, April 29, 1970. E1-3.

International Cable Protection Committee. **Cable Database. Eastern Pacific.** http://www.iscpc.org/cabledb/epac_page.htm Accessed June, 2001.

Jones, James, 1974. **Hawaiian recall.** Harper's 248 (February 1974): 27-31.

MacCaughey, Vaughan, 1918. **Eastermost** [sic] **Oahu.** Paradise of the Pacific. December, 1918. p. 49-51.

MacDonald, Gordon A. & Will Kyselka, 1967. **Anatomy of an island, a geological history of Oahu.** Honolulu: Bishop Museum Press. 36 p. (Some of the information is out of date, but this is still a useful short guide written for the lay person.)

MacDonald, Gordon A., A.T. Abbott & F.L. Peterson, 1983. **Volcanoes in the sea, the geology of Hawaii.** 2nd ed. Honolulu: University of Hawaii Press. 517 p. (The standard text on the subject.)

Markrich, Mike & Bob Bourke, 1994. **Hanauma Bay, an ecological guide for children of all ages.** Honolulu: Ecology Comics/Illustrated Science Press. 51 p. Art by Billy Kanae. (This entertaining "comic book" for children is full of fascinating details and stories of interest to adults as well.)

Moberly, Ralph & George P.L. Walker, 1987. **Coastal and volcanic geology of the Hanauma Bay area, Oahu, Hawaii.** Geological Society of America

Centennial Field Guide Cordilleran Section, 1987. p. 5-12. (A self-guided
geological tour of southeast O`ahu prepared for geologists attending a conference
in Honolulu.)

Sterling, Elspeth P. & Catherine C. Summers, 1978. **Sites of Oahu.**
Honolulu: Bishop Museum Press. 352 p.

Conservation and Regulations

Gulko, David, 1999. **Hawaiian coral reef ecology.** Honolulu: Mutual Publishing. 244 p.

Hawai'i. Division of Aquatic Resources. Dept. of Land and Natural Resources.
Hanauma Bay MLCD, O'ahu. http://www.state.hi.us/dlnr/dar/mlcd/pages/hanau-
ma.html Accessed June, 2001

Fishes

Hawaii's state fish. Humuhumu-nukunuku-a-puaa *(Rhinecanthus rectangulus).*
http://www/geobop.com/World/NA/US/HI/Fish.htm Accessed August, 2001.

Hoover, John P., 1993. **Hawaii's fishes, a guide for snorkelers, divers and aquarists.**
6th printing (revised). Honolulu: Mutual Publishing. 183 p.

Randall, John E., 1996. **Shore fishes of Hawai'i.** Honolulu: University of Hawai'i
Press. 216 p. (The most authoritative guide to Hawaiian fishes.)

_____, 2001. **Review of the Indo-Pacific surgeonfishes of the genus** *Ctenochaetus.*
Indo-Pacific Fishes. In press.

Randall, John E. & Helen A. Randall, 2001. **Review of the fishes of the genus
Kuhlia (Perciformes: Kuhliidae) of the Central Pacific.** Pacific Science 55 (3):
227 256.

Ryan, Tim, 1984. **Humuhumu winner of popular vote for Hawaii's state fish.**
Honolulu Star Bulletin. Dec. 5, 1984 A1.

Titcomb, Margaret, 1972. **Native use of fish in Hawaii** (2nd ed.). Honolulu:
University Press of Hawaii.

Invertebrates

Hoover, John P., 1999. **Hawai'i's sea creatures, a guide to Hawai'i's marine
invertebrates.** Honolulu: Mutual Publishing. 366 p.

Veron, J.E.N. & Mary Stafford-Smith, 2000. **Corals of the world.** Townsville, Australia:
Australian Institute of Marine Science. 3 v.

Turtles

Balasz, George H., 1980. **A review of basic biological data on the green turtle in the
Northwestern Hawaiian Islands.** In Grigg, R.W. & R.R. Pfund, eds. Proceedings of
the Symposium on Status of Resource Investigations in the Northwestern Hawaiian
Islands. Univ. of Hawaii Sea Grant Misc. Rep. 80-4. p. 42-54.

Hawai'i Preparatory Academy. **HPA/NMFS Sea Turtle Research Program.**
http://www.hpa.edu/TurtleTagging/TurtleTagging.html Accessed June, 2001

Hawai'i Volcanoes National Park. **Hawksbill turtle.**
http://www.nps.gov/havo/hawksbill.htm Accessed June, 2001

Pacific Whale Foundation. **The Hawaiian green sea turtle.**
http://www.pacificwhale.org/childrens/fsgreensea.html Accessed June, 2001
_____. **The hawksbill turtle.**
http://www.pacificwhale.org/childrens/fshawksbill.html Accessed June, 2001

Turtle trax, a page devoted to marine turtles. http://www.turtles.org. Accessed June,
2001. (A good informative website with plenty of accurate information on the
Hawaiian Green Turtle.)

Coralline Algae

Bernatowicz, A.J. **Algal foray at Hanauma Bay.**
http://www.botany.hawaii.edu/botany/guide/field3a.htm Accessed June, 2001
Doty, M.S. **Marine algae of Honaunau and Kealakekua bays.**
http://www.botany.hawaii.edu/botany/guide/field18.htm Accessed June, 2001
Keats, Derek W. **An introduction to coralline algae.**
http://www.botany.uwc.ac.za/clines.htm   Accessed June, 2001
Magruder, William H. & Jeffrey W. Hunt, 1979. **Seaweeds of Hawaii, a photographic identification guide.** Honolulu: Oriental Publishing Co. 116 p. (Out of print, but available online at http://www.coralreefnetwork.com/marlife/stepath/Default.htm Accessed Sept. 2001.

General

Castro, Peter & Martin E. Huber, 2000. **Marine Biology,** 3rd ed. Boston: McGraw Hill. 444 p. (A lively, easy-to-read general introduction to marine biology for college students.)
King, Liysa, 1990. **Hanauma Bay, an island treasure.** Aiea: Island Heritage Publishing, 96 p. Photography by Don King. (Beautiful photographs and interesting Hawaiian lore.)
Pukui, Mary Kawena & Samuel H. Elbert, 1986. **Hawaiian Dictionary, rev. and enlarged ed.** Honolulu: University of Hawaii Press. 572 p. (Hawaiian fish names and cultural use of fishes.)
Scott, Susan, 1993. **Exploring Hanauma Bay**. Honolulu: University of Hawaii Press. 90 p. Photography by David Schrichte. (A good practical guide to snorkeling in the bay, with great underwater photos.)
Thomas, Craig & Susan Scott, 1997. **All stings considered: first aid and medical treatment of Hawai'i's marine injuries.** Honolulu: University of Hawai'i Press. 231 p. (The most comprehensive and authoritative guide on the subject.)

INDEX OF SCIENTIFIC NAMES

INDEX OF HAWAIIAN NAMES

INDEX OF TOPICS AND COMMON NAMES